HIGHLAND EXPERIMENT

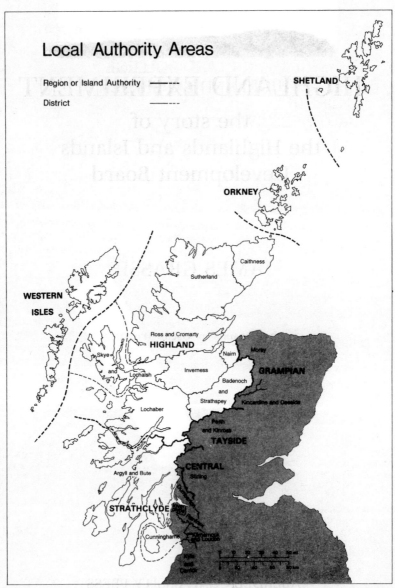

Local Authority Areas

Region or Island Authority ———----
District ————----

SHETLAND

ORKNEY

Caithness

Sutherland

WESTERN
ISLES

Ross and Cromarty
HIGHLAND

Skye
and
Lochalsh

Nairn   Moray

Inverness

GRAMPIAN

Badenoch
and
Strathspey

Kincardine and Deeside

Lochaber

Perth
and Kinross

TAYSIDE

CENTRAL
Stirling

Argyll and Bute

STRATHCLYDE

Cunninghame

Kyle
and
Carrick

Published by permission of HIDB

HIGHLAND EXPERIMENT

the story of
the Highlands and Islands
Development Board

JAMES GRASSIE

photographs by Oscar Marzaroli

ABERDEEN UNIVERSITY PRESS

First published 1983
Aberdeen University Press
A member of the Pergamon Group
© James Grassie 1983
Photographs © Oscar Marzaroli 1983

British Library Cataloguing in Publication Data
Grassie, James
Highland experiment
1. Highlands and Islands Development Board
I. Title
354.4110082′09   HC257.S4

ISBN 0 08 025765 8 (hard)
ISBN 0 08 028473 6 (flexi)

PRINTED IN GREAT BRITAIN
AT THE UNIVERSITY PRESS
ABERDEEN

THE BEGINNING

'We had to begin by ordering the paper clips,' was how Bob Grieve described the Highlands and Islands Development Board's start in life. Its first chairman, he was met on the doorstep of the board's Inverness office on his first morning in the job by a fisherman from the west coast in search of assistance.

Given what many saw as an impossible job by Parliament it was a unique experiment in regional development policy in the UK. How it tackled that task in its four central activities provides the substance of this book.

CONTENTS

ILLUSTRATIONS

The photograph used in the jacket design is of the Standing Stones, Callanish

PREFACE

According to its statute the board was to have no more than seven members, the majority of them full-time, including the chairman. All would be appointed by the Secretary of State for Scotland.

In the period to 1980 there were essentially three boards, the first led by Bob Grieve (1965–70), the second by Andrew Gilchrist (1970–5), and the third by Ken Alexander (1976–80). David Dunbar-Nasmith, latterly deputy chairman, was persuaded to act as chairman in the interim between Ken Alexander's departure and the arrival in February 1982 of Robert Cowan.

The board hired its own staff and for the bulk of the period to 1980 organised them in the following divisions: Fisheries, Industrial Development and Marketing, Land Development and Tourism as the four development teams; Administration, Finance, Information Services and Planning and Research as the servicing divisions.

Within limits set by the Scottish Office, the board devised its own procedures and policies. Broadly speaking, the function of staff was to research and prepare policy initiatives for the board's consideration and decision; to examine and bring forward to the board individual development projects; and to investigate applications for assistance and prepare them, with recommendations, for discussion and decision by the board.

Normally the board met in full session every two weeks. Outside that formal machinery it was capable of acting in emergencies with full-time members taking decisions which would be ratified at the next full meeting. It was, and of course remains, responsible to the Secretary of State for Scotland and works to him through the Scottish Economic Planning Department, on the annual vote of which its budget is carried.

Because it was seen by its founders as a special solution to a special problem, the board was given a unique package of powers; it could give financial assistance—by way of grant or loan or equity—to any enterprise which, in its view, would assist the development of the region; it could acquire land, compulsorily if necessary; it could set up businesses; and it could build factories.

To Wilma, Neil and Gillian

Together these opinions presented a fairly daunting challenge to the infant board which, if it wished to encourage the industry, would have to defeat that view, held in the higher reaches of the Scottish Office, as well as carve a niche for itself alongside the existing statutory bodies, the Herring Industry Board and the White Fish Authority. The HIDB accomplished both very quickly. That success was due almost entirely to Prophet Smith, a full-time member of the board who had been given the fishing portfolio: he had come from the headquarters of the Scottish Agricultural Organisation Society. He was not prepared to accept the conventional wisdom, placing much greater emphasis on the lack of capital.

With a rapidity which was to become part of the board's own nostalgia, discussions were held with the Department of Agriculture and Fisheries for Scotland, both statutory authorities as well as fishermen's representatives and those of local authorities; a proposal was prepared and submitted to the Secretary of State on 7 February 1966—within a hundred days of the board formally coming into being. A month later Willie Ross, Secretary of State, gave the scheme his blessing.[2] Based on the knowledge that the waters around the Highlands and islands could cope with more intensive fishing without endangering their future stocks, the board's plan was to build twenty-five vessels, at a cost of £750,000 over five years, for new entrants to the industry. Grant was to be provided by the Herring Industry Board or the WFA as appropriate and the board would offer a loan which, with the entrant's own contribution, would match the price of the boat.

The board decided to direct the scheme, in the main, towards increasing the local fleet at Stornoway. By the end of 1966, twenty-six applications had been made, and of these nine had been selected. Leaving as little as possible to chance, the board also made arrangements for training the new skippers and commissioned a standard design for a 54-foot stern trawler which they would make available to successful candidates. Macduff Boatbuilding won the first order under the scheme but it was from the yard of J & G Forbes of Sandhaven that the launch of the first completed vessel—appropriately named *Alpha*—took place on 22 June 1967. By then the main elements of the board's approach to the industry were present, at least in outline. The burden of putting it into practice fell on the shoulders of James Lindsay, who had been appointed to the board's four-man projects team in the middle of 1966. Prior to that he had worked in paper manufacturing and had no experience at all of the fishing industry. Fortunately for his employers, and for Highlands and island fishermen, he was a quick learner.

Policy was stated simply. 'Fishing is very important where it really counts,' Grieve wrote in the first report, 'and that is largely in certain islands and other communities where the tradition is still strong and where processing of the fish can be the basis of a land rooted industry.' Later, in the section dealing with the industry itself, the board pointed out that its concern was 'to ensure that an increasing share of the resources of Highlands and islands inshore fishing waters is derived by locally based fishing vessels manned by men resident in the Highland and islands'.[3] Inelegant phrasing, perhaps, but it defined the intention fairly precisely.

Progress with the main fisheries development scheme was steady. Almost coincident with the *Alpha* hitting the water, the board sought the Secretary of State's approval to extend the programme to Orkney. With less speed on this occasion, taking until the end of November, he agreed. By July 1968 the first ten vessels under the original scheme were fishing.

Since one of the board's intentions was to bring new blood into the industry, training was crucial. A three-pronged approach was adopted. By arrangement with the appropriate manufacturers, engineers on the new vessels were given short training courses at their works. The other members of the crew were given spare berths on existing vessels and, following the launch of the new boat, the crew trained as a working unit under one of the four training skippers the board had engaged for the purpose.

The method of financing the purchase, of course, was also helpful to younger applicants. Though they were expected to have a financial stake in the boat the board did not stipulate what it should be; in the event this allowed men with relatively little capital to own their vessels. Some were able to take charge of an asset costing some £25,000 to build, in return for putting as little as £1000 of their own cash on the table.

From early 1967 the board also offered help in the purchase of second-hand vessels. Here it was not concerned with size and thus found itself financing 22-foot lobster boats as well as a 92-foot purse seiner. The provision of loans in this way revealed an unsuspected demand and, for that first year, the board limited its approvals to twenty-five cases.

That the board was determined to follow a comprehensive approach was clearly evident. In the board's first year much of the approach had been foreshadowed. Then the board already had invested in processing, asked applicants under its development scheme to produce at least one tender from a Highland boatyard, begun a survey of harbours in the region, undertaken a visit to Denmark to examine fish farming and had looked at the marketing of lobsters from the Uists.

Nowhere was its comprehensive approach more quickly apparent than in Shetland. Events there proved Prophet Smith's argument that the main brake on development was not, as suggested in some circles, an absence of initiative and application but the lack of capital. The islanders moved speedily to take advantage of the board's financial resources.

The results were dramatic. A later report commented, 'The high level of prosperity in Shetland, based on fishing and knitwear industries has become almost a byword; but to those who knew Shetland in the circumstances of a decade and more ago, the present situation contains something unreal and miraculous. In contrast to the former depression, unemployment and emigration, the two main industries are at full stretch, labour not easy to get, and the drift of population arrested. . . .'[4]

By then (1971) the fleet of full time vessels had grown from 58 to 84 and the landings of fish had grown from 357,000 cwt in 1965 to 547,000 cwt. In fish processing there were 15 factories which employed up to 600 coping with a yearly throughput of 27,000 tons.

Processing also had been an early priority on Lewis. Since the board was directing its investment in new boats towards the Western Isles it was vital that onshore facilities at Stornoway should be able to match the bigger supplies of fish that were in prospect. The Herring Industry Board had a freezing plant and cold store close to Stornoway's quay. Employing only eight, it had limited attractions for local fishermen and, in theory at least, because of the Herring Industry Board's remit could deal with only herring.

On 14 June 1968 Prophet Smith announced the board's plans to take over the factory and expand it, investing some £100,000 over three years. He took some pride in the fact that it was the first time the board had gone into business for itself and he assured the local community that the project would be run 'as a fully commercial concern'.[5]

As the board saw it, it was a move which would maximise the benefit of the board's investment in boats. Taking control of the plant on 1 July, the board quickly appointed an experienced manager, christened the enterprise Gaelfish and got down to business. New equipment was installed and production lines were rearranged. White fish, herring, prawns and scallops were its raw material. The board did not expect to make an early profit and realised that if it were to make any at all in later years, then Western Isles fishermen had to cooperate by landing their catches at Stornoway.

From the fishermen's point of view, of course, that would depend on the prices Gaelfish was able to offer. This was a constant source of friction and was not really solved until the board was beginning to feel the influence of the new Conservative Government which, after the 1970 election, forced the board to sell Gaelfish just when the project was moving into the black. Curiously enough the purchaser was a Norwegian company, Rolf Olsen. It

Figure 2. Salmon Farm, South Uist

was not curious in the sense of being the first time the board had found itself dealing with an investor from Scandinavia. By then it already had assisted two processing interests from Norway, one of whom had established a plant in Inverness while the other had seen an opportunity at Mid Yell, Shetland for a shellfish cannery. The interest of the Olsen deal was that it established a link between the fishing industry in the Western Isles and Norwegian capital which was to be strengthened on a much bigger scale before the decade was out.

Meanwhile the board did not need to look overseas for capital to strengthen the region's boat-building industry. Such enterprise was no stranger to the Highlands and islands, the very nature of which had demanded from the earliest times that those who wished to live there had to learn how to make seaworthy craft.

The early boat builder held a respected position in his local community, but he was bound by his local market, a limitation that his descendants in the twentieth century had not broken. In the early 'sixties most yards in the Highlands tended to produce traditional vessels destined to be used in local waters by local crews. There was no reason for them to do otherwise until the board revealed its ambitious plans to invigorate the fishing industry.

It took its first tentative steps in 1967 by helping Andersons of Stromness to exhibit at a show in London. By the following year it had provided finance to the same company so that the company could expand its facilities. Andersons won the contract for the first boat to be built under the board's scheme by a Highland yard. Though the vessel in question, *Kildinguie* was launched in good time at the beginning of 1969 the Stromness yard suffered several setbacks, including the death of its owner, and eventually went out of business.

The same fate did not befall the other boatbuilder with whom the board became associated in 1968. Campbeltown Shipyard in which the Lithgow Group was to be involved, was set up that year and intended to offer repair services as well as new vessels. The attraction to the board was that the yard was to build in steel and would be the first in the Highlands to do so. In addition it held out the prospect of seventy jobs. Within a year the yard was complete and working on its first orders. At that time the board reported that, under its varous schemes—to the main development scheme it had added the capacity to aid the buying of dual purpose boats of up to 30 feet and of special seaweed boats of up to 15 feet—it had been able to give work to nine builders in the region. Their location ran from Hamnavoe in Shetland to Wick and Argyll. 'It is almost certain,' the board reported, 'that some of these yards would have had to reduce their scale of operation quite drastically and perhaps even go out of business had it not been for the stimulus provided by the board.'[6]

There was a certain amount of satisfaction at board headquarters. 'The sea, the old highway and support of the region,' Prophet Smith recorded, 'is once more playing a vital role in the life of island and coastal communities. The board's investment . . . has provided or saved almost 1000 jobs; a worthwhile achievement in four years.'[7]

Unable to resist a chance to counter the pessimists who, prior to 1965, had doubted that real dividends would come from investment in fishing, he argued that the new vigour apparent in the fishing communities 'should erase the impression in the minds of so many people, who claim to be authorities on the mental and physical attributes of the islanders, that the inhabitants of these areas are not as capable as people elsewhere of vigorously pursuing a fishing vocation. The proof is there for all to see. It has now been accepted that a sizeable fishing industry . . . can be built on sound commercial lines in the Highlands and islands, from Shetland to Kintyre, with processing and other facilities ashore to service it.' The board's task was to nurture the development and it was preparing to discuss with Government and other interests 'the best means of ensuring that the next stage of development (was) as successful as the first'.

He had an impressive list of deeds to back up his optimism. Eighteen of the vessels under the main scheme had been launched and were fishing, aid had been agreed towards the purchase of 67 second-hand boats and of 30 new dual purpose vessels while ten for seaweed collectors had been built. The board then still ran its own processing factory in Stornoway and had invested in seven other similar but independent enterprises.

The board also recorded its first hesitant steps to invest in fish farming. 'The western seaboard of the region,' it argued, 'with its sheltered sea lochs and temperate waters of the Gulf Stream is ideally suited to the techniques now being developed for marine fish farming.'[8]

At Ardtoe the White Fish Authority was doing a great deal of work with the commercial market very much in mind. The board supported that research and provided substantial funding to the authority. But it also had other prospects to pursue. One, at Kinlochbervie, failed in an attempt to break through the existing frontiers. The idea, promoted by a former skin diver in the Royal Navy, was to farm lobsters on the seabed. Specially built pens were meant to protect the young shellfish from their natural predators and, at the same time, provide a cage convenient to the skin-diving farmers.

Scottish Sea Farms at Loch Creran was a much bigger project and used methods which already had been tested. Based on work carried out in Ireland the scheme set out to hatch, rear and fatten oysters for consumption at home and overseas. Costing over £100,000 it was expected to create around 70 jobs in about six years. Work began on the site before the end of 1969.

At Loch Sween mussels were being grown on rafts, a method which then was claimed to be new in Scotland. The final product had been smoked and test marketed with encouraging results.

As the seventies opened there were over thirty employed in this infant industry throughout the Highlands and islands. But the board realised that problems could arise from the need for a high level of expertise in the operation of fish farms and from the constant risk of disease which could wipe out an entire stock very quickly.

Meanwhile the board focused its main attention on proposals to extend its programme in the traditional industry. Its report, *Of Special Importance*, was the opening shot in that campaign. There was some bravado in its claim that 'the board's involvement in active promotion of the fishing industry has increased to the extent where we think it is true to say that the board is now regarded in the Highlands and islands as the principal agency for the development of the industry both at sea and ashore,'[9] but it was on that basis that it brought forward new plans for discussion with DAFS and the statutory authorities. These plans sought to build on the programme carried out in the previous five years. They also contained a proposal which, if implemented, would have tilled new ground.

The board saw its provision of training for new skippers as essential to the continued success of its investment in fishing. 'It is not sufficient simply to make money available for the purchase of boats,' it argued in its 1969 report. Training and after-care for recruits to the industry were of great importance. This was perhaps true in many other areas but it was 'doubly important in the Highlands and islands where the failure of an individual enterprise (could) so drastically affect the outlook and morale of an entire community'.[10]

At that time the Scottish Education Department was consulting local authorities in the north east of Scotland about a proposal to concentrate education for fishermen in one school in the Aberdeen area. The board was not totally convinced that the suggestion made sense, believing it would focus on the needs of the trawling industry rather than of the inshore fleet which was predominant in its own area where, it considered, separate requirements had to be met.

These views the board conveyed to the SED which, though it gave them a sympathetic hearing, argued that cost considerations ruled out the setting up of separate training centres. But the board persisted.

'There are already over 2500 men engaged in full time fishing in the Highlands and islands,' it declared, 'and this number may well increase as we implement our plans for developing the industry. Because of this and our own capital investment in the industry and the speed at which the technology of fishing is changing, we think it is essential to ensure that the men who crew the boats are equipped with the necessary skills. We have, therefore, resolved to seek the necessary authority to make provision at our own hand for fishery training in the Highlands and islands.'[11]

Among its major proposals to continue developing the industry the board included one to purchase a training vessel which it would deploy itself. Though happy enough with the training programme it had run up to that point—it then employed five training skippers—it was not entirely satisfied that the best results were being achieved; training on board a working vessel, for one thing, could offer recruits lessons in bad as well as good habits.[12]

Another qualification was offered by Willie Russell who pointed out that the existing arrangement did not really provide 'the necessary controlled and systematic conditions for training younger entrants'. He went on to argue, 'the answer . . . seems clearly to be in the provision by the board of a training boat of (its) own for training purposes. This would enable the board to ensure both higher and more uniform standards of training and the inculcation of good methods and habits.'

Initially the board's case made good headway, managing to win the approval of the SED. The Scottish Development Department, its sponsors, however, took a different view, rejecting the proposal because it considered the board's existing arrangements adequate to the purpose.

At that time it was felt by some board staff that another consideration in the department's mind was the sad experience of the *Adalla*, the 92-foot purse seiner in the purchase of which the board had assisted in 1967. Though not a training vessel the *Adalla* had been seen as a means of encouraging the spread of that kind of fishing in the Highlands. But the project ran into some very rough water and failed, forcing the board, with the approval of the Scottish Office, to write off nearly £24,000.[13]

Such a misfortune could not have made the passage of the board's proposal any easier but when the SDD eventually turned the proposal down it effectively relegated training in the board's list of priorities for several years. In the interval the board had commissioned Willie Russell to review the progress of the fisheries development scheme. His conclusion gave the board all the encouragement it needed to invest in the future of the fishing industry.

This caused no surprise. As a former senior official in the Scottish Office, Willie Russell had acted as the board's friend at court and had encouraged it in many of its activities. His remit had been widely drawn. Not only was he asked to conduct a review of but also to assess the current lines of its development 'and make comments, suggestions or recommendations as seem appropriate'. He accomplished his task as a result of a brief but intense period of research, investigation and consultation. Russell's conclusion and recommendations were extensive. In its central objective of expanding the fishing industry the board, he considered, had been success-ful, its activity having had a 'substantial impact on the economic and social life and well being of the area'.

A 'notable' gap in the board's shore development policy occurred on Lewis and there, 'there (was) an urgent need to explore and work out means of developing a shore industry' on the island 'involving, if possible, development of more fishing on the west side . . . with appropriate facilities' there and with expanded processing in Stornoway. Linked to this was the suggestion that 'the larger and longer-term possibilities of industrial fishing with special reference to Orkney/Shetland and the Outer Isles (especially Barra) should be investigated and planned for'. 'Fishermen in Stornoway, Russell added, interested in that kind of fishing should be encouraged 'with a view to strengthening the fish-processing industry there'.

Not all, of course, was sweetness and light. He detected a 'degree of ignorance or suspicion' about the board's fishing policy, particularly on Skye. There was a need for 'improvement in the communication between the board and the communities' and 'some adjustment of the board's organisation' was called for.

This was a recommendation on which the board took no immediate action. What Russell seemed to be suggesting was that the board's staff ought to be organised in a way which reflected more the distinct political geography of the Highlands and islands and less their own functional priorities. This, in theory, would enable an official to deal with a community across the whole range of the board's activities rather than have to call in colleagues whenever inquiries passed out of his own disci-pline. The appointment of staff to posts away from its Inverness head-quarters went some way to meet that objective as did a later move which organised the board's large financial team on a geographic basis.

In the short term he supported the board's moves to seek the Government's agreement to extend their activities. 'Taking into account,' he wrote, 'the needs and potential of the various communities and of the Highlands and islands as a whole, and other relevant factors, including the (admittedly broad) assessment of fish stocks, and the scope for the WFA and HIDB to assist the increasing number of experienced fishermen in the area, I conclude that there is still substantial need and scope for continued involvement by the HIDB. I accordingly recommend a programme for the next five years to strengthen the Highland fishing fleet further by some 250 fishing boats.' This programme was to consist of 40 new boats under an extension to the board's original fisheries development scheme, 100 dual purpose boats and 110 second hand boats. The cost to the HIDB he estimated at £3.3 million in loans and grants and to the WFA and HIB some £600,000 in terms of grants.

All of this was sweet music to the board's ears. It had submitted its proposals to the Scottish Office in September 1970 only months after the general election which had brought the Conservatives back to office. The new team at St Andrew's House, under Gordon Campbell as Secretary of State, needed independent evidence that the board's approach was the right one, particularly in view of the uncertainties surrounding the UK's entry into the European Economic Community. Though it involved delay, and a temporary extension to the board's scheme, Russell's report gave them that. And in February 1973 Campbell gave his blessing to the extension the board sought. This programme was to run until 1977 at an estimated cost of £4 million.

By the time of the Secretary of State's approval, the boatbuilding industry in the region was in better shape to take the opportunities which undoubtedly would be presented by the new programme. The board had invested around £250,000 in the industry and had taken other steps to underpin it. In addition to its requirement that applicants under its major scheme of boat provision should seek at least one tender from a yard located in the Highlands and islands, it insisted that, as far as the purchase of smaller boats was concerned, its help would be conditional on the vessels being built in the region.

Prospective boat owners found that their choice no longer was limited to traditional craft in the traditional material, wood. Ferro-concrete and steel were now possibilities; a small yard using the former had opened for business in 1972 at Scrabster while the first steel-hulled vessel in the board's scheme, the *Crimson Arrow*, had been launched from the new yard at Campbeltown in February 1970. During that year also the board, in the aftermath of the collapse of the Anderson company at Stromness, succeeded in attracting Halmatic, which used glass reinforced plastic in its construction of boats, to Orkney.

That pattern of steady expansion was destined to be broken. As in much else, the chief agent of the change was the leap in oil prices in 1974. For that year the board recorded that the sharp increase in the costs of new boats meant that only one order was placed for a vessel under the fisheries development scheme.[14] In the following year the lack of interest was remarked once more while the board's total assistance to the industry as a whole fell by over 18 per cent to £1.6 million.

Ironically, these steeply rising costs, in fuel as well as construction provided the board with additional justification for its plans to exploit industrial fishing in the north east Atlantic. Initially based on the availability of blue whiting in these waters the board's proposals were relevant not only to the Western Isles but to the UK as a whole.

Research voyages, which had begun in 1967, had proved the existence of a very large stock—some estimates put it as high as fifteen million tons—of blue whiting in the waters to the west of the Hebrides. Most of these had been undertaken by DAFS and the Ministry of Agriculture, Fisheries and Food. The board added its mite in 1975 by chartering two Peterhead-based vessels, MFV Shemara and MFV Fairweather, to carry out a four-week exploratory voyage.

An unpublished report[15] set out the board's thinking. Arguing that the potential of the fishery was of world importance—the annual catch could double the total UK landing of all species—it suggested that its chief importance was 'as a source of raw material for reduction to meal and oil'.

At that time the UK was importing on average between 350,000 and 400,000 tons of fish meal annually at a cost of around £50 million. According to the report, exploitation of the blue whiting could cut the UK's import bill and perhaps lead to a 'situation in which this country could become a net exporter of meal'.

To gain that opportunity meant an investment in new harbour and reduction facilities in the Western Isles. The board proposed that these should be located at East Loch Roag in Lewis and Northbay on Barra and had commissioned relevant engineering studies in both areas, which were ideal because of their proximity to the fishing grounds—an advantage that would be crucial in a period when, as the report remarked, 'concrete (would be) cheaper than fuel oil'.

It was an attractive proposal which had been argued persuasively by Jim Lindsay to the board which had endorsed it enthusiastically in February 1975. Such were the ramifications and implications of its plans, that the board took the unprecedented step of setting up a special project team with Lindsay temporarily relieved of his broad responsibilities with its fisheries division, at its head. He pulled in staff which gave the team financial, planning and engineering expertise and got down to the task of putting flesh on the board's strategy.

Evidence of the team's effort was available in a speech made by Ken Alexander in Aberdeen on 24 September 1976. Illustrating changes in the fishing industry he pointed out that in the ten years to 1976 the Scottish inshore fleet had decreased by 46 vessels on the coast between Berwick and Inverness, increased by 20 in Ayrshire and Bute and by 225 in the area served by the board. In the same period the trawler fleets at Aberdeen and Granton had lost around 20 per cent of their vessels. 'The one outstanding negative feature,' he argued, 'is that there has been little or no attempt to exploit the waters to the west of the Hebrides, waters very much more heavily utilised by the vessels of other nations.' Imports into the UK outweighed exports by a factor of four, a substantial deficit which would not be improved by the recent agreement with Iceland which lost the UK some 90,000 tons of fresh fish a year.

> To achieve any substantial improvement to the balance of the fish trade it will be necessary to tackle the problem on a number of fronts (he claimed). It would be desirable to reduce the dependence of the UK on imports of fish meal, to improve both the volume and the value of exports and to reduce the dependence on high cost imports of canned goods. Reduction of the country's dependence on imported meal and the increase in the quantity of exports can only be achieved by increased landings, and increased landings can only be achieved by utilising new species such as blue whiting, and by Scotland making greater use of the conventional fisheries in the sea area to the west of the Hebrides.
>
> Once a 200 mile exclusive economic zone is in operation, it is probable that the largest part of the sea area involved . . . will be open equally to all nations within the EEC. Without some very definite efforts, both commercially and politically, it is unlikely to say the least that our fishermen will obtain a reasonable share of the available tonnage. It is vital that our negotiators and those they are negotiating with should understand the economic and social magnitude of the decisions they are taking. From Brussels, or even from London, what is at stake may look like a very few jobs measured against the scale of European economic problems. But the fishing and fishing-related employment in many of our communities is a very high proportion of the total population. For example, at Mallaig the figure is 23 per cent, at Lochinver 14 per cent, in Scalpay 11 and in Shetland 8. It is also important, however, that the fishing industry should not allow its concern with the national exclusive zone to completely overshadow the opportunities which will open out with the establishment of the EEC exclusive zone of 200 miles. The expulsion of all those non-EEC countries who are currently scooping up fish within this zone will create opportunities which, if our industry does not grasp them, will certainly be taken up by our European associates.

The development of the resources to the west of the Hebrides, he stated, required a definite and directed effort and the board was playing a major

role in generating the initial momentum. 'The key problem is not one, at this time at least, of responding to pressure from the existing fleet for better facilities, or of achieving shore employment by improving the commercial infrastructure of marketing for an existing operation. Rather it is one of persuading UK fishery interests of the need to extend their operations into this area at a time when they have just recovered from a most severe depression, and on the other hand of providing facilities on shore which will attract EEC as well as UK vessels to land there.'

Focusing on the latter he explained that in the Outer Hebrides the two best sites were at Northbay, Barra and East Loch Roag, Lewis and that these should be developed in parallel. Advancing reasons for that argument he went on,

Firstly, the distance between the two places is approximately 95 miles by sea. Concentration on one site effectively adds 190 miles of steaming both to the north and to the south for a single vessel's journey to and from the fishing grounds. A fleet of 40 vessels making four such journeys every fortnight is the equivalent of once round the world, and in the long term concrete will be cheaper than fuel oil.

Secondly, concentration on one location would not thereby save the complete cost of one entire harbour installation, since it would be necessary to provide additional berthing space at the single location in order to handle the same traffic. If two piers were created instead of one, then the cost is virtually the same, while if one pier were extended further into deeper water there would inevitably be an increased cost per linear foot which would offset most of the financial advantage in the single site.

Thirdly, while reduction factories should be able to operate profitably on the tonnages brought in over the main blue whiting season, they will clearly wish to extend their operations over the largest part of the year. To do this they will handle tonnages of other industrial species which are found in the waters surrounding the Western Isles but which, as far as is known, are present in much more modest quantities than the blue whiting and much closer to shore. They will accordingly be fished by vessels similar to the present class of 60 ft to 90 ft inshore vessels whose economic range on this fishery will be limited. For example, a 65 ft trawler catching pout to the south of Barra cannot afford to run with them to the reduction factory at Stornoway.

The most difficult part of a development to achieve, is the initial steps. It is unrealistic to postulate investment in pier facilities in the absence of any concomitant commercial interest in operating from that location. And there may well be difficulty also if the first commercial developments are obliged to carry the financial burdens of certain inputs, for example pier, water and electricity, which will themselves provide the attractions for future investment. But these are just the kind of 'Catch 22' situations which development boards are created to resolve and the HIDB is now busy at work on these problems.

It was a confident note on which to end given that the board's project team was not sweeping all before it. Lindsay always had recognised that the central problem would be to persuade the British fishing industry that the north eastern Atlantic held a resource which would be profitable to exploit. That was proving to be the case, a situation which eventually forced the

Figure 3. Trainee skippers, Lews Castle College

board to look overseas for support and to secure interest, once more, from Norway.

A/S Stokfisk was in the business of drying and selling fish, running two factories, of which the newer was at Vigra, an island near Aalesund. Its principal was Per Stoknes, a curt, brisk Norwegian who had designed and patented a unique automated drying process. Since 1965 the company had built up demand for its products in Scandinavia and elsewhere and was looking for a site for expansion overseas because it reckoned that new international fishing agreements would weaken the access of the Norwegian fleets to their traditional grounds.

In contact with the board since 1974, Stokfisk had concluded that Breasclete on East Loch Roag met its requirments. Efforts to interest UK firms, notably the John Wood Group of Aberdeen, in sharing the prospect failed and the board decided that if progress were to be made then it would have to take the initiative.

Its eventual plan was to build a 45-metre pier at Breasclete giving direct access to a new factory of some 20,000 square feet which it would also build. It would set up a company, in which initially the Norwegians would have a minority holding, to operate the fish processing and drying plant.

Per Stoknes was to be project manager at a salary of £6000 a year plus expenses. A new UK company, in which he would be the controlling share-holder, would enter into a management contract with the operating concern. This arrangement would provide for a management fee—at a minimum of £40,000 a year for the first three years of production—which would be based on a formula, the object of which was to enable Stoknes and his associates to acquire control of the operating company in a relatively short period of time.

In return he would make available all drawings for the factory, which essentially represented a transfer of technology proved in Norway to Lewis. He also would be the fulltime managing director of the operating company with responsibility for buying, production, liaison with the marketing and management company, technical matters, accounting and data processing—jobs which he carried out for A/S Stokfisk and which would be defined in the management contract.

At the outset he also would purchase £30,000 of ordinary shares and would undertake to provide a further £70,000 of finance at a later date, both amounts being subject to the consent of the Bank of Norway.

Crucial to the success of the venture, of course, was adequate supplies of fish. The board estimated that in its third year of operation the factory would require over 5500 tons in roughly the following proportions: saithe,

730; tusk, 200; blue ling; 300; white ling, 1560; blue whiting, 2400; and mackerel/herring, 500.

Considering that this could represent a fishery competitive with others available, the board approached leading trawling companies in Scotland and one of them showed interest in landing at Breasclete. It also decided to provide finance and training towards achieving the operation of two or three line vessels in the Western Isles.

It was estimated that up to 36 fishermen could earn their livelihood by carrying the specified catches to Breasclete where the factory itself would employ 34 full time and up to 15 part time. Construction would require about 30 men. A survey of the Breasclete area suggested that such resources would be available and that, indeed, there was a clear need on employment, demographic and social grounds for development to take place. If it took the shape of a fish drying factory of the kind proposed, there would be a stream of benefits—in incomes, in the saving of transfer payments, in increased tax and local rates—of some £12 million over fifteen years. In the same period the UK's balance of payments would benefit to the extent of approaching £30 million.

Taken as a whole the board's approach to exploiting the potential of the fisheries to the west of the Hebrides was its most ambitious initiative to date. Although it was in many respects a natural progression from its earlier work in the industry it contained the spark of imagination and foresight characteristic of enterprise which breaks new frontiers.

The strategy had been a long time in the making. Work on it began under the enthusiastic leadership of Sir Andrew Gilchrist who had been the UK's ambassador to Iceland at the time of the first Cod War and who, therefore, was familiar with the politics of fish. He considered that, though the trawlermen of Hull and Grimsby had been the victims of the disputes won by Iceland, the inshore fishermen of the Highlands and islands had gained in opportunities. It seemed proper to him, therefore, 'to intensify the successful assistance programme which the board was operating'.

After leaving the board he wrote,[16]

The gainful activities of the inshore men, however, were menaced by the almost incredible error made by the British Government when joining the Common Market in accepting the right of fishermen from the partner countries (our main competitors) to fish right up to our shores.

A ten year 'derogation' from this deadly concession enabled the inshore fishermen to fish happily on in the seventies while Hull wasted to death; and it was sedulously put about that long before the ten years came to an end the up-to-the-shore concession would be negotiated out of existence. (And don't forget that the assurances for the most part were gladly accepted by the fishermen themselves.)

The first opportunity to deal with the question arose at the Wilson 're-negotiation' and I pressed on the Scottish Office the need to give a high priority to restoring the position on fish. The failure to insist on any such modification was a serious warning signal, so much so that I reached the private conviction that nothing significant would be done and that the concession to the Common Market represented a most serious menace to the British inshore fishing industry.

If Iceland had killed the big trawlers, the Common Market would cripple the remainder. It was scarcely possible for an appointee like myself to say in public not merely that the optimism of Ministers (of either persuasion) was ill-based, but that it was simple political dishonesty (though I said it plainly once I had left the board).

All I could do was to relate my conviction on this point to the enthusiastic interest then being taken by Prophet Smith and James Lindsay in the potential East Atlantic fishery where we had geographical and economic though not legal advantages; and to press for its financing and development not merely on regional but on national grounds. It was too big for the HIDB on its own; and the national element is still missing.

By the time Sir Andrew handed over the chairmanship of the board to his successor, Ken Alexander, the board's strategy was set and its first proposals to implement it had been devised. Contained in two detailed documents[17] (Hebridean Fisheries: 1 and Hebridean Fisheries: 2) they were submitted to the Secretary of State at the beginning of 1977, requesting his approval to the construction of piers at Northbay and Breasclete, and to the setting up of the fish drying plant, with its associated company, at the latter.

Throughout the process the board had kept the newly formed Western Isles Islands Council in close touch with progress. For its part the council, led by its convener, Donald Macaulay, was unstinting in its cooperation and assistance. Early in January 1977 the board for the first time published details of its plans for Breasclete. It did so in the course of a series of meetings in Lewis on January 11 and 12. Ken Alexander led a group from the board who discussed with crofters and landowners the land which the project would require and who met representatives of the Islands Council. Also on their programme was a public meeting at the school hall in Breasclete organised by the local community association. Both the community and the council gave their enthusiastic backing to the project

Almost precisely six months later the Secretary of State, Bruce Millan, authorised the construction of the pier and the purchase of the land. His announcement had been preceded 24 hours earlier by a further series of meetings between board representatives and local interests. This time the board's team was led by Gordon Drummond, a newly appointed member who had been given responsibility for the Breasclete project.

In the school hall that night Per Stoknes was on hand as were samples of the dried fish he hoped the new plant would produce; a film, dealing with other projects in which the board had been involved, was shown and villagers were able to meet its makers, Oscar Marzaroli and Allan Campbell McLean, who had been commissioned to produce another focusing on Breasclete; detailed accounts of the proposed plant were given and Gordon Drummond undertook to keep the community in close touch with progress.

The Secretary of State's decision was welcomed by Ken Alexander who declared that he saw the board's strategy 'as the best long term prospect for employment in the Western Isles'. Emphasising once more that the board was determined to try to ensure that the principal benefits would accrue to local people, he added, 'Clearly a certain amount of re-equipping, particularly with larger boats, may be necessary if the local fishing fleet is to play its full part in the catching side of developments. Fishermen have already shown their interest through their response to a new series of courses at Lews Castle College [in Stornoway] for the Department of Trade certificates needed for the operation of larger vessels. This is the first step and they are taking it positively'.[18]

Having approved the board's overall strategy and given it the necessary approval to go ahead with the acquisition of land and the building of the 45-metre pier (at a cost of more than £350,000), the Secretary of State was unlikely to balk at the last hurdle and, at the beginning of August, he duly removed it, authorising the board to build the factory and invest in the new company which was to run it.

The price was £1.2 million—$700,000 for the factory, the balance for the company. Deputy chairman of the board, Rear Admiral David Dunbar-Nasmith, explained that site works for the plant would begin shortly and that the board hoped to have it in production by the end of the following May. 'This means that the construction schedule will be very tight but, given the active cooperation of all those concerned, we should make it,' he said.[19]

Per Stoknes was equally optimistic. 'Our factory will require about 5500 tonnes of fish a year from the grounds to the west of the Hebrides,' he told the press. 'We have no worries about securing these supplies, provided prices are fair, and neither should there be any concern about damage to long-term stocks.'

Lewis Stokfisk Ltd, 75 per cent owned by the board, 25 per cent by a new Scottish company to be formed as a subsidiary of the Norwegian interests, was to run the factory, with Per Stoknes as full-time managing director and a part-time chairman and a financial director appointed by the board. The board subscribed for 300,000 of the 400,000 ordinary £1 shares and for all of the 100,000 £1 preference shares.

As work began, attention was focused on the need to ensure adequate supplies of fish to the processing factory. In its submission to the Secretary of State the board had stated that it planned to use some of its normal training and financial effort to achieve the operation of two or three line vessels from the Western Isles. 'There is still a considerable tradition of line fishing in this area,' it had argued, 'and (the board) has reason to believe that a move in this direction would be welcomed by certain of the younger skippers. . . . It is clear that the Norwegian system of lining which is designed for the pursuit of white ling as a main target should be followed, but the board is under no illusion that the provision of even two or three vessels and the training of their crews will necessarily be an easy matter. However, on this occasion there is time on the side of the board since the proposed factory would not be in production until spring of 1978 and would not be in full production until 1980.'[20]

As events transpired the board needed all the time available. In June 1978 it announced that it was helping finance a Lewis family to acquire the *Anni Elisabeth*, a Scandinavian vessel, and to equip it with automated lining. Willie John MacLeod and his three sons were to own the boat which would be skippered by Robert MacKinnon who then was completing his training at Lews Castle.

In September the board revealed it was backing a group of interests in the setting up of the Breasclete Fishing Company Ltd to convert and run a 115-foot Aberdeen trawler, the *Grampian Crest*. Involved in the enterprise were two line skippers from Anstruther, Alex Anderson and George Barclay; the vessels current owners, George Craig & Sons Ltd of Aberdeen; and Lewis Stokfisk. The board took a fifth of the company's £100,000 share capital and also provided finance for the conversion. That work was expected to be completed by the end of October.

Most of the crew for the vessel would be experienced line fishermen from the east coast who were prepared to give new recruits training on board. Rear Admiral Dunbar-Nasmith welcomed that aspect of the development. 'We have great faith in their skill and enterprise. . . . It is heartening too, that they have decided to pass on their knowledge by offering training berths on the *Grampian Crest*,' he said. 'I am certain they will be well used.'[21]

By this time the *Anni* had made four voyages with encouraging results. The whole project seemed ready to take off when the factory opened in October. But it opened its doors only to trouble. For the following twelve months it staggered from uncertainty to uncertainty.

Its chief difficulty was that it could not obtain adequate supplies of fish.

The owners of the *Anni Elisabeth* were not happy with the prices they were offered and, because of that, were loath to exchange the traditional Scottish practice of catching varied species to protect themselves against the vagaries of the market for the Norwegian custom of targeting on the particular fish the potential buyer wanted.

On several occasions instead of heading for Breasclete they burned more fuel in running to Aberdeen and Fleetwood in pursuit of higher prices. One such journey cost their insurers £50,000 for the repair of the hull, damaged in taking a short cut through the Sound of Barra on a run to the English port.

The factory meanwhile tried to get supplies from Norwegian vessels but for these had to offer a premium, for their skippers, by taking their catches to their home market, would get an additional subsidy for doing so. Relations between the Norwegian management and the community deteriorated. Heated words—and on one occasion a blow—were exchanged in the local bar. Losses mounted. Lord Mansfield, Minister of State at the Scottish Office, formally opened the factory in the early summer of 1979 and when it was visited a month later by Prince Charles, special arrangements were made to ensure that sufficient fish was landed to have the factory working.

By then its quality controller, Alastair Fraser, had resigned because of disagreements with his superiors and particularly with his managing director, Per Stoknes. Though it owned 75 per cent of the company the board seemed reluctant to intervene or to attempt to build bridges between the workers and management and between management and the community. It stood aside in September when 10 employees were sacked at short notice. The following month Per Stoknes summarily dismissed Donald John MacLeod as production manager.

In November the *West Highland Free Press*, under a front page headline, 'What's wrong at Breasclete?', reported that a meeting called by the local community association had concluded that there was no local confidence in the management of Lewis Stokfisk. Chairman of the association, Donald MacLeod, said that the discussion at the meeting—to which Alistair Fraser had contributed—had amounted to 'a terrible indictment'.[22] A few days later Willie John MacLeod of the *Anni Elisabeth* said that the vessel would not be returning to Breasclete until there had been a change of management.

Though this was a period in which, Gordon Drummond later confessed, the board saw disaster looming,[23] it did not move publicly. Away from the public forum Jim Lindsay was trying to solve the basic problem—the lack of fish supplies. Arguing and persuading the owners of the *Anni Elisabeth* was no easy task but it was relieved unexpectedly by the one ray of hope to emerge—the willingness of Faroese boats to land at East Loch Roag.

The first tied up at the Breasclete pier in November but the board was not confident enough to face the whole community until two months later. Then Ken Alexander led a small group to a meeting in the school hall. To his audience he gave a frank account of the factory's difficulties as well as its mistakes but stressed that the board still had confidence in the project. This was based on the fact the Lewis Stokfisk had entered into arrangements with enough UK and foreign boats to meet the plant's requirements for a year. Emphasising that these were arrangements, not contracts, he also made it clear that the factory would want to deal with the vessels' bycatches as well as its own target species.[24] The meeting rekindled a spark of confidence. The board's judgement was that the factory would be back to full capacity in five to six weeks. Within a matter of days the *West Highland Free Press* carried a picture on its front page of busy workers unloading fish.

But other difficulties were to arise. In April Per Stoknes sacked the man appointed to succeed Donald John MacLeod before his three-month probationary period was up. 'The factory is running fine,' he said, 'and it seems everything is under control.'[25] Problems also broke out on the converted *Grampian Crest* where there were tensions among the crew. These were beyond resolving and the vessel landed few catches at Breasclete.

In all the board provided financial assistance amounting to over £350,000 to the company which owned the vessel. The initial investment, by way of equity, loan and grant, took place in 1978 with a second injection, amounting to £135,000, being made in February 1980. Eight months later the *Grampian Crest* was tied up, with the proprietors going into liquidation and the board allowing for a loss of £260,000 in its accounts for 1980–1.

Meanwhile 1980 seemed to be the year in which the plant at Breasclete began to look as if it could realise the hopes which had accompanied its birth. Though Lewis Stokfisk recorded a loss of over £308,000 for the year the board was able to report that supplies of fish had improved considerably; the company, however, had been forced to buy a proportion at high rates from Norwegian boats. Catches from the *Anni Elisabeth* 'were generally satisfactory with a larger proportion of ling and tusk being caught, while arrangements had been made for further supplies'.[26]

But the company's financial situation was deteriorating. The board gave extra help in 1981 which, together with an earlier tranche of finance in

1979, totalled £575,000. Trading losses were expected to reach £708,000 by the end of the year. Much of the sorry tale was given to the House of Commons Committee on Public Accounts in the spring of 1982. The MPs were not impressed and in their report concluded that the board 'appeared to have continued to commit support to (the Breasclete factory) beyond the point at which a dispassionate re-appraisal should have led it to call a halt'. They suggested that the SEPD and the board conduct a thorough review of the latter's arrangements for the financial control of projects. In particular they wanted the review to cover 'the arrangements for the initial appraisal of investment opportunities, and particularly the quality of the board's internal monitoring arrangements, in addition to the arrangements for reporting progress to SEPD on projects which the departments have approved'.[27]

The MPs report looked damaging but the board took it fairly calmly. It had been living with the problem for nearly three years, it knew its every move had been examined rigorously by Scottish Office and the Treasury before being approved, and, before the report was published, it had called in receivers to Lewis Stokfisk. Its confidence in its strategy remained unaffected and it maintained that commercial interest continued to be expressed in opportunities at Breasclete. Meanwhile it had secured the promise of a fish meal factory at Ardveenish on Barra which would give life to the second phase of its strategy. These plans, which had been proposed by the Hull Fishmeal Company, were endorsed in August by the community on Barra.[28]

Fish farming

In its first report the board devoted all of two sentences to fish farming. 'We are keeping under review the potential of our area to sustain fish-farming enterprises,' it stated. 'In this connection a visit was paid to Denmark in August by two members of the board's staff to assess the potential for fish farming in the Highlands and islands on the fresh water pattern as practised in other countries.'[29]

Fourteen years on six pages were required to record the board's activities in the industry during 1980. By then its investment in fish farming had grown to nearly £6 million, of which about a quarter had been directed towards research and development. Finance from private sources amounted to more than £9 million and about 250 people depended for their income on full-time employment in the trade.

The possibilities had been recognised early. Bob Grieve, in the course of a meeting with the first group of Conservative MPs to visit the board, had told them it was one of his priorities. It was to be prosecuted vigorously in the years ahead.

No skilled detection was required to see that much of the coastline of the Highlands and islands was suited ideally to fish farming; the deep sea lochs, the ample supplies of fresh water and, of course, the presence of the favourite of the geography textbooks, the Gulf Stream, were all obvious advantages.

What were needed to tap such potential were steady application of energy and finance, and a willingness to take risks.

Through time, of course, dividends from the former helped reduce the need to apply the latter. The board went about securing them in several ways.

Under the persuasive influence of Prophet Smith and of the reasoned cases brought to them by their fish farming team, headed by Bill Mackenzie, board members willingly accepted that much of the investment they approved would be consumed by research and development. Their annual subvention to the White Fish Authority at Ardtoe fell into that category and created an acceptable precedent.

Eventually they saw the potential benefits that could flow from the building up of a body of expertise and skill outside the statutory organisations. This they encouraged by providing finance to Fish Farm Development Ltd. which established itself in Argyll. Having an independent source of advice on tap was important not only to the board but also to the many budding practitioners in the trade. Psychologically it also confirmed the area's pre-eminence in fish farming.

More important in the quest to cut risks to a minimum was the need to find a stable supply of disease-free ova. An outbreak of disease in 1972 which had brought a farm close to final disaster persuaded the board to take matters into its own hands.

Later that year it announced that it was to build its own trout hatchery at Moniack, several miles north of Inverness, expressing the hope that it would make an important contribution to the future development of trout farming throughout the UK.

'. . . At the moment Highland trout farms are in an extremely vulnerable position,' the board told the press, 'depending on overseas supplies of certified ova which could not always be relied upon'. The new hatchery, it contended, could ensure stringent control and regular inspection of ova.[30]

Built and stocked in 1973 the hatchery, using sterile water from boreholes, was able, within three years to sell all the ova it could produce. By then the board had taken a third fundamental step to reinforce the infant industry by arranging with the Inverness Technical College to run a prototype training course for youngsters keen to work in fish farming.

Out of that trial, which ran for a few weeks early in 1977, came the first full course which began in August 1977. Thirteen students took advantage of the scheme which, according to the board, was aimed at producing 'a competent fish farm operative rather than an employee of managment calibre'.[31] By 1980 thirty-nine youngsters had passed through the year-long course and the board was considering setting up a permanent training facility on the west coast.

For those who completed the course there were ample opportunities. In 1980 alone the board had trebled the finance it had offered the industry in the previous year. Since its cautious beginning it had assisted 56 fish farming businesses—39 of which were involved in salmonid production, 15 in shellfish, one in eel farming and one in contract research work.

In October Ken Alexander took a sanguine view of prospects. 'Fish farming is a rapidly growing sector,' he said. '. . . Over the next two decades the number employed in this activity should increase from the present level of approximately 200 to somewhere in the 750 to 1000 range.'

Notes

1   *The Scottish Economy 1965 to 1970, a Plan for Expansion* Cmnd 2864, January 1966
2   HIDB, First Report, 1965–6, p 20
3   Ibid. p 19
4   *In Great Waters* Special Report 7, HIDB, 1972, p 44
5   Press release 31/68, HIDB, June 1968
6   *Of Special Importance* Special Report 2, HIDB, November 1966, p 19
7   Ibid. Foreword
8   Ibid. p 24
9   Ibid. Introduction
10 HIDB, Fourth Report, 1969, p 53
11 Ibid. p 54
12 *In Great Waters* p 55
13 Ibid. p 56
14 HIDB, Ninth Report, 1974, p 66
15 *The Blue Whiting* Special Report 14, HIDB. This document—which laid the foundation for a new fishery strategy—was printed and ready for distribution but the board decided not to publish it

16 These comments are from a note written by Sir Andrew Gilchrist to the
    author
17 These documents outlined the board's strategy for exploiting the waters to
    the west of the Outer Hebrides and, though never published, were
    circulated widely among local and central authorities
18 Press release 27/77, HIDB, June 1977
19 Press release 34/77, HIDB, August 1977
20 Hebridean Fisheries, HIDB, 1976, para 2.33
21 Press release 44/78, HIDB, September 1978
22 *West Highland Free Press* 23 November 1979
23 *West Highland Free Press* 7 March 1980
24 *West Highland Free Press* 7 March 1980
25 *West Highland Free Press* 4 April 1980
26 HIDB, Fifteenth Report, 1980, p 62
27 Committee of Public Accounts, 21st Report, Session 1981/82, HC 301, 13 July
    1982, HMSO
28 *West Highland Free Press*, 7 August 1982
29 HIDB, First Report, 1965–6, p 22
30 Press release 68/72, HIDB, September 1972
31 HIDB, Twelfth Report, 1977, p 70

TOURISM

The soft option

Providing peace and recreation for the rest of Britain was a familiar role for the Highlands and islands. There had been early travellers, like Boswell and Johnson, but it was not until the nineteenth century that visitors came in significant numbers to holiday in the area. As early as 1808 a special guide book was advertised in the Inverness newspaper to cater for that incipient taste which really began to exert an influence as a result of Victoria's love affair with the Highlands. The board, therefore, was on the firmest of grounds when it described tourism as one of the main props of the regional economy. Despite that general agreement, prior to 1965 the industry had been left pretty much to its own devices.

Nationally the development and promotion of the industry was the responsibility of the Scottish Tourist Board, then a non-statutory organisation which was chronically short of funds and expertise.[1] From its headquarters in Edinburgh it ran one office in Inverness. For the rest the industry was in the hands of well-meaning individuals who, generally, neither had the time nor the experience to deal adequately with its problems. For tourism there was no strategy and, even if there had been, there were no means by which to carry it out.

For the Highlands the only guidance came from the White Paper on the Scottish Economy which had seen tourism being developed 'both to assist consolidation in some of the main centres and give a supplementary income to the dispersed population engaged in primary and service industry'.[2] No organisation, the board realised, could tackle even that limited remit but itself. Early in 1966 it appointed Mike Robinson, already experienced in the travel trade, as the member of its project team to devise a strategy which would fulfil the remit. Prior to coming to Inverness, Robinson spent time in the US—at his own expense—studying the Tennessee Valley Authority and its approach to development.

The board, of course did not await the outcome of Robinson's work before it acted. At the prompting of the Scottish Economic Planning Council

it decided to tackle the question of lack of accommodation in the Western
Highlands and islands. On 14 June it submitted to the Secretary of State a
formal proposal to provide new hotels in these locations and, following his
approval in principle six weeks later, set out to study the feasibility of five
hotels which would cost a total of £1 million.[3] This scheme was to provide a
continuous thread in the board's tourism work running all the way
through to 1980.

In its first year it also responded to requests for financial assistance from
various quarters. By the end of 1966 it had approved nearly £300,000 to
projects as varied as guest houses and caravan sites. It had invested money
in promoting sand yachting in Caithness and in sea angling from Ullapool
and had supported an STB publicity campaign to the extent of £5000. It had
managed, too, to take its first steps in the field of winter sports, the development of which was to occupy a great deal of its energies in later years. The
Cairngorm Winter Sports Development Board was one of the first
organisations to knock on the board's door in a search for funds, in this
case to help increase its chairlift capacity.

The board obliged by means of a short term loan at the end of January
1966. Three months later a new company, Cairngorm Sports Development
Ltd, was launched in order to allow new capital to be brought into the
venture. The board provided £25,000 by way of debentures and Grieve
became a director of the company. By then Robinson had set out his
proposals. They were comprehensive, touching on accommodation,
facilities, publicity and promotion, and research and marketing. Vital to
realising their objective was the setting up of a specialist team of staff who
had relevant expeience. Before the end of 1966 the board had approved
both the strategy and its staffing implications.

Members decided, however, to give the task of implementing the plan
not, as was expected, to the man who had researched and devised it, Mike
Robinson, but to Ian Skewis who, for some months previously, had been
working closely with John Robertson, the board member then responsible
for Moray Firth Development as well as for the tourism portfolio. Dismayed
by this early example of internal politics and patronage, Robinson resigned
shortly thereafter, becoming the first official to leave the board's
employment.

Skewis, whose expertise was in transport matters, very quickly made his
presence felt. The plan which he inherited had four main objectives: first,
to lengthen the tourism season; second, to increase both accommodation
for tourists and their knowledge of it; third, to bring about an improvement
in hotel and catering standards; and, fourth, to encourage an extension of

tourist facilities and to improve the means of publicising them. Progress on all fronts was not slow to appear.

An advertising campaign to attract holidaymakers to the region in 1968 was launched. It was the first of its kind, exclusively devoted to the Highlands and islands and it was the board's hope that it would 'provide the basis for a steady increase in the number of visitors in future years over an extended season and that this in turn (would) encourage further investment for the development of the industry'.[4] It was a classic and trusted recipe—increase the pressures of demand and growth in supply will result. In addition the board saw tourism as the one industry from which it could obtain worthwhile dividends relatively speedily.

Fortune smiled on the board's efforts. International travel was setting out on a period of spectacular growth from which the Highlands would be bound to benefit while, in 1968, the first year for which a special promotional campaign had been devised, the weather throughout the summer was glorious. In these conditions, it was not surprising that the expenditure on brochures and advertising was seen as worthwhile investment. From that initial season, it became a fixed part of the board's tourism work, rising in ten years from the first hesitant £5000 contribution to the STB's programme to over £250,000.

That willingness to mix it in the market place with international competitors—exemplified by the £45,000 the board spent on Highland Fling, an exhibition held aboard the RMS *Clansman* at Tower Pier, London in January 1969[5]—exercised its own pressure. It nurtured the development of new products which, properly packaged, could be sold in the market and it helped force-feed the industry in the region on a diet of change.

For 1969 a new marketing scheme was devised. Called Highland Holiday Ticket it offered discounts on behalf of 300 businesses, from hotels to shops, during the off-peak months—an idea that was being pursued also to strengthen the winter sports business in the Spey Valley. Such initiatives were predicated on the belief that, as holidaymakers came in increasing numbers, the trade in the Highland and islands would be able to respond. 'Tourism will develop successfully,' the board argued, 'only if local tourist associations are organised on a strong professional basis.'[6] The day of the volunteer relying on a shoe-string budget was all but over while that of the area tourist organisation was beginning.

For the 1969 season a network of thirteen such organisations was in place. Each had an elected council which was responsible for policy, the implementation of which was the job of their full-time salaried tourist officer. The role of the organisations was to run information centres, provide a local booking service, publish promotional material and organise festivals and other entertainment.

The board rightly set great store by creating this structure for the industry. By 1970 there were 14 organisations in existence: Mid Argyll, Kintyre and Islay; Dunoon and Cowal; Oban, Mull and District; Fort William and District; Skye; Wester Ross; East Ross; Inverness and Loch Ness; Spey Valley; Sutherland; Caithness; Orkney; Shetland; and Western Isles. The running costs of each organisation were met by the board which estimated this would require around £40,000 a year. Contributions to the budget also came from the local authorities and from the local industry itself. In addition the board undertook to provide finance towards the provision and improvement of tourist information centres.

For the first time anywhere in Scotland the holiday business was in the hands of professionals. The structure also afforded the Highlands and islands the opportunity to coordinate activities as well as policies; regular meetings were held of all tourist officers while provision was made, too, for exchanges between representatives of the councils which ran each area organisation. Through time the area structure assumed a growing number of functions. The organisations became involved, under the board's aegis, in exhibitions, produced brochures, accommodation guides, ran advertising campaigns, and promoted festivals. They also presented the board with a useful channel to the views of those directly involved in making their living from the industry.

Their chairmen, along with the board member responsible for tourism policy, formed the Highlands and Islands Tourism Council which, in 1976, took on the task of producing, with financial support from the board, the main brochure promoting the holiday attractions of the region as a whole. Though much of the real work continued to be carried out by board staff, the council brought two main advantages.

First, it gave the Highland tourism industry another voice. It had representatives on the Scottish Tourism Consultative Council, for example, and the Scottish Civic Entertainment Association. It also was able to lobby bodies and organisations, such as the major petrol companies, to seek decisions favourable to the development of the Highlands' holiday trade.

Second, because of its direct involvement in the region's main advertising campaign—and the need to be geared to respond to inquiries generated by it—it was able eventually to provide additional employment. In 1980 it established a distribution centre at Golspie in Sutherland and staffed it for its first season with fourteen temporary officials. It hoped in the longer term to provide permanent employment.

Figure 4.   AA Chalet development, Carrbridge

By then there were fourteen area organisations in existence—employing 150, of whom a third were full-time—and the board was able to describe them as 'an increasing significantly mechanism for development'.[7] They had led the way, for example, in running the Book-a-Bed Ahead Scheme which was applied later throughout Great Britain and, in 1980, were introducing a voluntary classification scheme for accommodation establishments. Underlying their growth was the continuing problem of finance. The board failed to persuade the trade itself to make the contribution to the organisations' budgets of which the board thought it capable. Local authorities, too, particularly from the mid-seventies onwards when they were faced by growing Government pressure to cut spending, were reluctant to increase their share.

In 1978 all the organisations took part in a coordinated drive to attract new trade members. 'This was successful,' the board reported, 'both in producing a useful number of new members and in increasing the awareness of local people of the work of the organisations and the importance of tourism to the local economy.'[8] Evidence that such a view was shared by the other main participants in the industry was demonstrated by their willingness to contribute to the area organisations' income. In 1971–2 the board had carried the main burden, providing 62% of the total £116,000 with a further 20% coming from the local authorities. A decade later the board's share of a much larger total (£822,000) was 37%; the local authorities 27%; the trade 24%; the balance of 12% coming from sales and booking fees.

By then the tourism boom that had begun in the mid-sixties was over. The Western Isles Tourist Organisation reported in August 1980, that bookings were down by 34 per cent on twelve months before.[9] Soaring transport costs and the strengthening pound, as well as the general economic recession were making Highland holidays less attractive. For a second year running the board, and the Scottish Tourist Board, had pressed the panic button and run secondary advertising campaigns costing around £150,000 each. Their intention was to reassure intending holidaymakers that, though petrol was in short supply in some places south of the Border, Scotland in general and the Highlands in particular were not suffering a scarcity that could upset holiday arrangements.

Playing key roles in the board's efforts were the network of tourist organisations which acted as a source of intelligence, and, of course, the board's marketing experience. The latter had been built up over a decade to produce a selling package that was at least as good as any in other parts of Britain.

The assumption by the Highlands and Islands Tourism Council of the general role had allowed the board to concentrate on promoting specific geographic and activity initiatives. This was a natural extension of the success it achieved in two particular spheres.

First was Travelpass, a ticket which offered tourists comprehensive travel facilities at inclusive prices. This fitted snugly with the board's broad objective of supporting public transport throughout its area as well as its narrower tourism policy. An integral part of the scheme, which by 1980 was being sold in the US and Europe as well as in the UK, was a comprehensive transport time-table. Though its accuracy was constantly in doubt— mainly because the board could never devise an administrative system that could cope with the vagaries resulting from the independence of many of the smaller transport operators in the islands[10]—it was a document which gathered for the board a great deal of public credit.

The second was the Highland Holidaycard. Providing the holder with discounts for accommodation, shops and a wide range of facilities, this was directed towards encouraging visitors in the off-peak months.

Throughout the seventies the board paid growing attention to broadening its contacts and encouraging the maximum exposure of the Highland industry in the international market place. In 1978, for example, it took representatives of 21 tourism concerns to meet nearly 150 travel agents in Germany, France, Belgium and Holland; and a further 15 to Germany, Denmark, Sweden, Finland and Norway. Out of that drive the companies took an immediate £400,000 worth of business as well as the prospect of more.[11]

Board staff themselves spent a great deal of time abroad, mainly in North America and Europe. In conjunction with the British Tourist Authority they attended workshops and exhibitions where they dealt directly with sources of new business for the Highlands. Not content with that continuing effort they persuaded the board to bring the international market to the Highlands. The board approved their proposal to follow the example of the Highland Crafts Fair and establish a platform from which the Highland holiday industry could sell its wares. The first Tourism Tradex International (TTI) was held in Aviemore in 1975 'to stimulate an increase in the area's tourism industry'.[12]

It was an ambitious endeavour to bring together the two sides of the market, the buyers and the sellers. There were 116 stands in the exhibition and these were visited by around 300 travel agents, a substantial number of whom came from overseas. Out of their exchanges came one deal which the board regarded as particularly significant; Tjaereborg Rejser, a Danish travel company, agreed to organise package holidays from Denmark using charter flights into Dalcross Airport. This was evidence that the Highlands were ready to compete in one of the fastest growing sections of the tourism market.

A second TTI was arranged for the following spring. It took place in Inverness and was attended by around 100 Highland businesses and 450 agents, 160 of whom came from abroad. Enough trade was done and enough experience gained to persuade the board that it should make TTI a regular, though not annual, feature of its marketing.

Its confidence seemed to be justified by the third fair, held in Inverness in 1978. Although the overall attendance was lower than the board wished, it produced business valued at over £2 million for the following year. Tjaereborg, in the interim, had expanded its interests so that it was running charters from Germany as well as Denmark. Because of that pressure the Civil Aviation Authority and Customs and Excise, at the urging of the board, improved facilities at Dalcross giving the airport an international dimension. That new doorway was important, symbolically and practically. The symbolism was obvious but behind it lay the fact that the region's tourism business was readier than it ever had been to match the demands of a market that was increasingly particular and discerning. This was especially the case in terms of accommodation.

Increasing both its quantity and quality throughout the region had been a constant priority of the board. It was to help meet this priority that the board had taken its first major initiative—the island hotel scheme—but it was a field, too, which was not always simple to cultivate.

At Minard Castle, Argyll, the board produced a board-assisted project which eventually foundered in a blaze of publicity. In Glencoe, where the board proposed in 1967 to build a caravan site at Achnacon, it uncovered such a hornets' nest of environmental protest that the scheme was dropped. That pattern repeated itself, though for different reasons, in the early seventies.

In 1972 the board unveiled its Holiday Cottage Scheme. Based on its belief that there was a 'large unsatisfied demand for self-catering holiday accommodation' the plan had three superficially attractive elements. If successful it would create an additional source of income for the region, add to its stock of accommodation and provide work for native building firms. The Royal Bank of Scotland would provide loans, and the board would provide grants, to those willing and able to build cottages for letting for the major part of the tourist season. This assistance would be offered only if the pre-fabricated cottage were manufactured in the region to a design approved by a special panel on which the board and the planning officers of the seven counties would serve.

Within seven months, designs from six local companies had been approved and the board itself had commissioned additional plans which were to be made available to any construction company already in, or prepared to set up a special manufacturing plant in the area. Widely promoted, the scheme had attracted over 10,000 inquiries by the end of the year, a few of them securing financial aid.

But already fundamental problems were becoming evident. The board had been correct in its assessment of the demand for such cottages but had been too hasty in putting its scheme together. The position of crofters, surrounded in their croft houses by a tangle of regulations, was unclear and the absence of an answer to the question of whether they could participate in the project provoked a rumble of discontent and criticism. Little attention had been given either to how to ensure that the cottages would be a genuine investment for holiday purposes rather than an acquisition for the sole use of the investor or his family. It was possible that area tourist organisations could take on a regulatory role but that would entail their assuming an extra burden to which perhaps they were not suited.

But the main problem, as was the case in other areas of Highland development, was land. A condition of the board's scheme was that not only did the applicant have to have the necessary plot for his cottage but also planning permission from the appropriate authority. The vast majority of those who responded to the board's publicity had neither. In February 1973 the scheme was suspended with no new applications being accepted unless they were from crofters, for whom special dispensation at last had been negotiated. 'At the end of the year,' the board reported, 'assistance had been approved for ten cottages, two of which are to be built by crofters.'[13] This did not mean that the pursuit of the self-catering market was ended. It clearly was growing and could not be ignored. Several individual schemes were assisted, one of the larger being that built by the Automobile Association at Carrbridge and opened in 1978. By 1979 the supply in the region amounted to 1860 flats and chalets able to provide around 10,000 bedspaces.[14]

The board met fewer problems and enjoyed greater success with another of its initiatives in the accommodation sector. This arose from the realisation that the bulk of visitors came to the Highlands by car and yet did not enjoy modern accommodation that had been built with them in mind. In response the board promoted a Tourism Inns Scheme. The company which finally exploited it eventually opened hotels in Inverness, Fort William, Ullapool and Wick.

As a whole, the tourism business was not reluctant to take advantage of the financial assistance that was on offer. New hotels appeared in Lerwick, Stornoway, Easter Ross, Aviemore and other places; older inns were modernised, guest houses put on extra rooms, and small bed and breakfast establishments improved their facilities.

Not all of this, of course, was achieved smoothly. Reservations existed inside and outside the board. In the main, these fed on the simple fact that, by 1973, tourism absorbed a great deal of the board's resources. By then, of the total £17.5 million the board had agreed to invest by way of loan and grant, over 30 per cent had been directed towards tourism ventures; and of that sum of over £5 million, approaching three quarters was grant. Internally there was a great deal of discussion about policy. Prophet Smith, whose field of responsibility was fisheries and agriculture, argued strongly for a change. He expressed the view that hotels were offered too much grant; tourism business was growing rapidly and investment in new accommodation carried few risks. Grants, therefore, ought to be trimmed and loans—indeed equity participation—ought to be increased.

It was a persuasive case, particularly because it coincided with two other factors. The first was the increasing pressure on the board's budget so that anything which could spread it over a wider range of activities would be welcome. The second was the feeling that the board should be able, on the basis of its experience, to be more flexible in its approach. It should be aiming at tailoring its assistance so that the most difficult areas would get the best financial package.

As a result of that debate the board attempted a more sophisticated way of investing in tourism.

In June 1973 Badenoch and the Inner Moray Firth were isolated as areas in which the board no longer would give grant towards accommodation and catering projects; in Oban, Fort William and Ullapool, the level of help on offer was cut to 40 per cent and the rate of grant available reduced to 25 per cent. In all other areas the total financial assistance (grant and loan) normally would not exceed 50 per cent of the total cost of the project—though exceptionally 70 per cent would be possible—while, within that, the maximum grant would be 35 per cent. Explaining the decision the board said '. . . it has become clear that some parts of the Highlands and islands have achieved a better rate of accommodation development than others and in these places we believe that good hotel and similar projects should be able to proceed with the help of loan assistance only, and in other parts with a reduced level of grants. Within the financial resources available to us, this cut back in assistance to these places should allow us to channel more help to stimulate development in other areas where there is great potential not being fulfilled, partly because of lack of capital.'[15]

The decision seemed straightforward enough but the complications inherent in it only became obvious when staff tried to put it into practice. It was important to know, for example, precisely where the boundaries of the various areas lay and, more importantly, the exact date when an application had been made. Uncertainties abounded and placed severe strain on officials as well as the board's processing procedures.

Despite these initial difficulties the policy was applied until 1976. By then there was evidence that even in the areas where the industry was strongly represented investors were unwilling to build new accommodation without the top levels of board assistance. The differentials were dropped and the board began once more to apply its rules uniformly throughout the region.

Externally tourism was seen as a 'soft option' providing only seasonal work and second class jobs. Grieve had been aware of that feeling in 1965 which, he claimed, contained the 'implicit assumption that any manufacturing industry, no matter how useless or dubious its product . . . is somehow more honourable than an industry which is designed to give a visitor a warm welcome, a comfortable bed and good food.'[16] If there was such a feeling the board then deplored it 'for we think that whether such employment involves work in a bed and breakfast establishment, a restaurant or a large hotel, it calls for personal qualities and professional skills of a high order'.[17]

But the view persisted and helped feed fears that an expanding holiday trade could damage the area's cultural heritage, particularly in the west and the islands. Angus Nicholson voiced these reservations in 1977 writing that tourism provided 'a useful boost to the local economy, but the Gaelic heritage and the Highland economy will never be as strong as they ought to be until less seasonal industries are established'.[18] But two years later the attitude still prevailed and it was seen as an obstacle to those who wished to invest in the industry. Alongside it, and supporting it, was the view, equally strongly held, that the board in its anxiety to encourage development gave unfair advantage to incomers compared to natives of the region. In tourism this opinion was not weakened by the influx of workers from overseas to fill jobs in catering and hotels. More importantly the opinion was supported by the issue of holiday homes, an apparently growing feature in many Highland villages where the locals held that the trend put housing out of the reach of their own youngsters.

This clearly was a social and political problem of importance and not only in the Highlands. In response the board, together with other Government agencies, commissioned some research into the question.

The Dartington Amenity Research Trust began work in December 1973 and produced an interim report the following May. That document, which revealed just how extensive were the gaps in information about second homes, provided the basis for further work the results of which finally were published in June 1977.[19] The study found that second homes—of which there were about 35,000 in Scotland—did not raise major national issues of scale or impact although problems could be created in the provision of local services and by the indirect effect of competition for housing. Action to control their development, if any were to be taken, lay mainly with the local authorities.

In any event the study was not directly relevant to the board's efforts in tourism where it was focussing on the need to improve the area's range of accommodation, adding to the stock rather than taking existing houses out of the local market. In that respect 1977 was an active year, with assistance being given to the Scottish Youth Hostel Association to improve the quantity and quality of its Highland properties—a relationship which had begun in 1970 with a board grant going to the new hostel at Torridon—and purchases in Harris and on Raasay which the board planned to develop as hotels.

The board also devoted considerable effort to the region's tourism facilities. It realized early that there was little point in attracting more and more holidaymakers without also trying to ensure that there was sufficient for them to do when they arrived. Fishing, climbing, hill walking and, to a lesser extent, sailing were traditional recreations in the Highlands and islands. To the contemporary market, however, they had limited appeal and, alone, could not support the increase in trade which was the board's objective. The board, consequently, sought out and supported opportunities in sand yachting, sub aqua diving, sea angling, pony trekking, golf, squash, ice rinks, cinemas, theatres, drama; financed festivals (sporting and artistic), concerts and tours. It also encouraged the development of 'wet weather' facilities, a prime requirement in an area as well known for the vagaries of its climate as its scenic attraction.

The board was fortunate in that there was an early conjunction between its anxiety to improve the region's facilities and an entrepreneur promoting a suitable project. David Hayes, the man in question, was keen to apply to Scotland the kind of interpretative approach to history and the environment which he had seen in national parks in the US. Fortunately he

Figure 5. Carloway, Lewis

had the financial resources with which to back his ideas. He found ready
support from the board which was prepared, too, to invest in the project.
The result was Landmark Visitor Centre at Carrbridge. Opened by the
Duke of Edinburgh in 1970 it suggested that imagination and good taste
need not be absent from investment in the tourism business. Costing
£190,000, the centre included an auditorium, with provision for films as
well as audio-visual programmes, an exhibition area, a restaurant and a
crafts shop. Well-landscaped and boasting a car park and picnic area among
the firs, it was a worthy winner of the 1970 Come to Britain trophy
awarded by the British Tourist Authority as the outstanding tourist
development of the year.

One of the attractions of Carrbridge as a location was that it lay within
the Spey Valley which, with its winter sports, enjoyed a season extending
for ten months. The same commercial fact spawned two later
developments.

The Highland Wildlife Park at Kincraig took advantage of the growing
public interest in wild animals and in the movement away from the narrow
confines of the traditional zoo. Its main focus was on a collection of animals
native to Scotland, including those which had been hunted into extinction
by man or nature. The park opened for its first season in 1972.

At Aviemore, Santa Claus Land owed everything to the commercial
instincts of the centre's management. Though it received the enthusiastic
backing of the board, it was to prove that lack of taste and imagination all
too often were part and parcel of attempts to cater for the holidaymaker.
Complete with bogus Santa and a North Pole provided by Walls, the ice
cream producers, it was the object of a great deal of criticism when it
opened in November 1976.

Later the board was active, too, outside the Spey Valley, supporting an
aquarium in North Argyll and the development of a visitor centre at
Ballachulish featuring the rise and fall of the area's slate industry.
Communities were encouraged to improve existing facilities so that the
board's finance found its way to unlikely spots like the small golf course at
Sconser in Skye as well as to more obvious locations like a new swimming
pool at Fort William.

A fresh holiday activity was opened up in the Great Glen through the
development of cruising on the network of waterways provided by the
Caledonian Canal. Private enterprise made the running but, with
substantial aid from the board, by 1980 there were seven companies hiring
out over 100 vessels and enjoying a 31-week season.

All of this brought other facilities in its train. The chief of these was a village of chalets, the Great Glen Water Park on Loch Oich-side. Growing interest also encouraged the board to devise a strategy for the recreational development of the Great Glen. The purpose of the strategy was to identify the facilities required and methods of achieving them through the application of resources from the public and private sectors. Coincidentally, with Argyll DC the board produced ambitious plans for the development of water sports for the west and south western seaboard. These envisaged a range of facilities from single mooring buoys to a causeway linking Oban and Kerrera. The price was estimated at around £10 million and the board appointed a new member to their tourism team to implement the strategy for the Great Glen and Argyll.

Two years before that policy was adopted in 1980, the board had attempted to use the steady growth of cruising in the Great Glen as a means of supporting another Highland industry, boat building. The original idea, outlined by Cliff Parr, the board's senior marine surveyor, was to design a new cruiser which could be built in the region's yards. Initially it was intended to offer the design to Highland boatbuilders so that they could compete for the cruising companies' demand for new vessels. Drawings of the cruiser, christened the *Highland Admiral*, were shown at the 1978 Boat Show at Earls Court and elicited a response which persuaded the board to commission the construction of a prototype for display and sale at the next show twelve months later.

Confusion of responsibilities among board staff, bad communications between them and outside participants and regular revisions of the budget continually threatened to undermine the project. But with only days to spare the prototype took its place in the centre pool at Earl's Court in January 1979. A year later the prototype and three other Highland Admirals had been sold.

Despite growing competition from other areas, typified by the lengthening season in the Great Glen, the Spey Valley remained the jewel in the crown of Highland tourism. Aviemore Centre, opened in 1966, had done what its proponents had suggested it would do—increase the business of surrounding hotels and guest houses. New accommodation was built at the centre itself so that, by 1980, in addition to the original cluster, an example of the architectural work of John Poulson, there were two new hotels as well as additional self-catering accommodation.

But the pre-eminence of the valley as a winter sports resort had not been unchallenged. Ben Wyvis in Ross-shire had been considered by some as a possible rival and the Scottish Tourist Board had drawn attention to the possibilities of Aonach Mor near Fort William. Lobbying on behalf of both areas was persistent. The board responded by undertaking more research. In 1975, in conjunction with Ross and Cromarty County Council, it produced a report on Ben Wyvis and in 1978 commissioned a fresh assessment of the winter sports market. The Highland Regional Council set up a working party to look at future development.

In 1980 the board felt able to 're-affirm support for a major expansion on Cairngorm and minor developments elsewhere in the Spey Valley'.[20] It claimed that there was a lack of clear evidence of demand and this raised doubts about the viability of Ben Wyvis. As for Aonach Mor, climatic and topographic conditions would make its slopes a 'difficult development option'. It kept that door open, however, by suggesting that 'more suitable slopes (might) be identified in the vicinity of Fort William'.

By then the board had invested over £4 million in Badenoch, much of it helping to improve the uplift on the ski slopes—which it had purchased from the Forestry Commission in 1971—build a restaurant on the summit and construct a road and car park to open up Coire na Ciste. As a result of its 1980 review further expansion was on the cards and the relevant proposals were to go to a public inquiry ordered by the Secretary of State the following year.

Notes

1   The Scottish Tourist Board took its present statutory form under the Development of Tourism Act, 1969. Its budget is provided through the Scottish Economic Planning Department which, for 1982–3, allowed for an expenditure of £8 million on tourism and its development
2   *The Scottish Economy, 1965 to 1970* Cmnd 2864, January 1966
3   HIDB, First Report, 1965–6, p 24
4   HIDB, Second Report, 1967, p 20
5   'It's been a resounding success—the calculated risk has paid off,' said Bob Grieve of Highland Fling (*Sruth* 23 January 1969) which had taken a taste of the Highlands to London. Over 40,000 visited the temporarily converted MacBrayne ferry during its ten-day stay on the Thames.
6   HIDB, Third Report, 1968, p 42
7   HIDB, Fifteenth Report, 1980, p 55
8   HIDB, Thirteenth Report, 1978, p 55
9   *The Scotsman* 26 August 1980
10 *Getting Around the Highlands and Islands* is described as a comprehensive guide to the area's transport system. It is, therefore, strictly speaking not a time-table. Estimates of its inaccuracy ran from 50 to 70 per cent so that complaints about missed transport connections were a regular feature of the

summer season at the HIDB's head office. But there was no way in which
such a publication could match its need for accuracy and advance planning
with the flexibility and informality of several services in the Highlands and
islands

11 HIDB, Thirteenth Report, 1978, p 52
12 HIDB, Tenth Report, 1975, p 57
13 HIDB, Eighth Report, 1973, p 56
14 *A Contemporary Account* HIDB, 1979, p 76
15 HIDB, Eighth Report, 1973, p 56
16 HIDB, First Report, 1965–6, p 2
17 Ibid. p 24
18 North 7, Issue 27, November/December 1977, HIDB, p 14
19 *Second Homes in Scotland*, a report for the Countryside Commission of
    Scotland, HIDB, Scottish Tourist Board and the Scottish Development
    Department; Dartington Amenity Research Trust, 1977
20 HIDB, Fifteenth Report, 1980, p 54

INDUSTRY

The problem is quite soluble . . . given the will

Manufacturing industry, wrote Grieve in the board's first report, was the third main prop of the Highland economy. 'We increasingly regard it as the most urgent of all relative to the immediate need to stem a substantial proportion of the emigration of talented sons and daughters from the Highlands and islands,' he went on.[1] The problems in forestry and tourism were of place and timing of development, level of investment and the communications to optimise them.

> But there has been no agency with the direct responsibilities and requisite powers to promote industrial growth in a thoroughly determined manner. . . . It is our clear duty to see that this most important and most deficient element in the Highland economy is furnished; it should be recognised by all that we must devote a substantial proportion of our effort to it.
> Manufacturing industry is very poorly represented in the Highlands and islands. Without it, the region will continue to lack any real possibility of a substantial enough rise in numbers to give credibility to Highland regeneration. Numbers are important in the justification or provision of all services internal to the Highlands and in major improvements in communications between the Highlands and the south. Modern industrial enterprises are absolutely essential in providing more of the kind of skills and initiative which will breed new enterprises and broaden the range of social and cultural leadership.

This was a fairly thorough statement of the philosophy which informed the board's efforts to get to grips with its most intractable problem. It provided Grieve with a base on which to define a three-pronged policy: the board would encourage the growth of industry wherever a developer showed a personal and specific desire to settle or expand; it would pursue, at the same time, a more methodical programme of building small industrial growth points in keeping with the possibilities of the west Highlands and islands; and it would do its utmost to generate major growth points, involving substantial increases in population, wherever the natural advantages of the area seemed to warrant it, with the Moray Firth being 'unquestionably the most important of these areas'.

The policy, though stated uniquely for the Highlands, was a direct descendant of the White Paper on Central Scotland published in 1963, in

44

which Grieve, as Chief Planner in the Scottish Office, had been a guiding influence. In setting out the growth point philosophy, the White Paper had broken new ground and contributed to the reputation being acquired by the Scottish Office for making a fundamental contribution to the development of regional policy in Britain. Essentially the notion was that public investment should be concentrated in certain favoured areas in order to make them more attractive to industry, thereby encouraging economic growth.

Applying it in a Highland context with any degree of consistency was to prove difficult. There were several reasons for this; first, the board's own limitations; investment in roads, schools, bridges, harbours and housing was a matter for others so that in these fundamental areas the board was destined to become merely the voice of yet another Highland pressure group. Further, it was not a planning authority. These powers remained entirely with the local authorities and they did not always share either the board's perceptions or its priorities.

Second was the nature of the board's ability to give and lend finance to industry. Though closely defined by the Scottish Office this never was subjected to a cash limit. Under these circumstances the board could not turn away applications for help on the ground that it did not have the money. Thus it could not exercise—and did not wish to exercise—any real control over the geographic source of these requests.

Third, and important throughout its first five years, was the fact that the industrial portfolio was ostensibly in the hands of John Rollo. Rollo had spent a lifetime in Highland affairs; at one time he ran four production units in the crofting counties and, as chairman of the Highland Fund, he had had a leading role in helping provide what really were character loans on easy terms to budding entrepreneurs the length and breadth of the Highlands and islands.

With that background he was uncomfortable with what he saw as the grandiose notions of growth areas and holding points. This was not surprising. In an article in *The Scotsman* in 1965, in which he had looked forward to the setting up of the board, Rollo had written: 'There is a tendency in certain planning minds to think in terms of concentration of populations around existing towns or large centres . . . with a view to factory development. This will be fatal for the Highlands because it will result in the complete destruction of the agricultural crofting population. Far more effective would be the concentration on the fostering and development of small factories located where the people are and have their homes and so allow them to have wage-earning work and work their crofts as an ancillary to give increased income.'³ In that view he was supported by many of the community's leaders who argued that the board should sow its seed over as wide an area as possible.

Rollo was a rugged individual blessed with unbounded energy. Throughout his spell at the board as deputy chairman, which he began in 1965 at the age of sixty-four, he commuted from his home at Foss in Perthshire, coming into Inverness daily by catching the overnight sleeper from London at Blair Atholl. While the train slept he dictated notes and memoranda ready for his secretary to tackle when she arrived at the board's office at nine o'clock. Unfortunately, his business life made it difficult for him to mould himself easily into the budding bureaucracy at the board's headquarters. He continued to act as he always had acted and ran his office as the one-man band he was. It was a source of conflict, manifesting itself periodically in a threat from the board's deputy chairman to resign. Responsibility for pursuing the big fish which could be landed on the shores of the Cromarty Firth was given to John Robertson, backed by a small group of staff.

Rollo pursued a string of smaller developments. Some, like Castlewynd Pottery, were destined to put down roots and flourish: others, like the fly-tying enterprise which took over a factory in Inverness and the business which moved to Barra to produce spectacle frames, were fated to have brief existences.

The dual approach to the question of industrial promotion gave outsiders the impression that the board had a split personality. The apparent glamour of tracking and attracting the industrial giants, tackled more often than not in the full glare of public attention and debate, sat ill with the chasing of the minnows to which Rollo devoted most of his effort. To many, including Scottish Office Ministers, the local press and An Comunn Gaidhealach, it was the latter job which the board had been set up to tackle. To them it was unacceptable that only John Rollo appeared to be doing it.

It was not until 1968 that the board moved to appoint staff with experience in the industrial field. Dugald Morrison, an industrial engineering consultant, arrived to give backing to the deputy chairman's efforts. He was given the assistance of one other member of staff. The contrast between principle and practice was vivid. It was a contradiction which could not go unnoticed. *Sruth*, the fortnightly bi-lingual newspaper published by An Comunn Gaidhealach, was critical. Its column 'The Industrial Scene' quoted one of the board's publications: 'The board see it as their clear duty to make sure that this most important and most deficient element in the Highlands economy (i.e. manufacturing industry) is furnished and have undertaken to devote a substantial proportion of their effort to that end.' It then added cynically, 'For once we can see just what these words mean and how important manufacturing industry is to the board. Out of a staff of 168 only two people (and the depute chairman) are involved in industrial promotion. A substantial proportion indeed.'[4]

That proportion did not change throughout 1969. Though Morrison and his colleague, James Abraham, were, like Rollo, engineers by training, they found it increasingly difficult to work with the deputy chairman.

Morrison attempted to introduce a more disciplined approach to the board's effort and set out to strengthen its contacts with Government departments and trade associations. He also tried to persuade Rollo and the board that more staff and more finance would have to be allocated to the task. But because there seemed to be a basic lack of accord between him and the deputy chairman he made no progress on that front. The tensions increased and finally erupted. At Easter 1970 Morrison came in to clear up his desk prior to going on holiday; he was interrupted shortly after his arrival by Rollo who told him that Bob Grieve, the chairman, would like to see him. An hour later Morrison had been fired.

The reason given was that he had exceeded his authority by committing the tenancy of a board factory being built at Inverness Airport to a potential developer without the board's approval. To several staff it hardly seemed a firing offence and the situation was not wholly irretrievable. Their cynicism was not overcome when, within four days of Morrison being sacked, Ian Skewis—at that point running the board's Tourism division—began to fulfil a remit given to him by the chairman of establishing what Morrison had been arguing for—a better staffed and financed industrial development division.

Before the month was out Skewis was telling the press, 'There will be a great similarity in my approach to that adopted by me to develop our tourism effort. We must produce the development opportunities, the sites, the factories, the finance and put these on display for sale. Because of our geographical position we must try to add something extra to our product and sell it that bit more aggressively.'[5] This was almost exactly what Morrison had been preaching but it was left to Skewis to put it into practice. Given a free hand by the board he raided every department—finance, administration, planning, tourism, publicity, management services and projects—to build up a staff of around twenty-four. It was the first major upheaval that the board's staff had experienced. Not all of them liked it, most of its senior members showing their anxiety by joining the board's branch of the Society of Civil and Public Servants.

The change was nicely timed. In common with those of the other full-time members appointed by the Secretary of State in 1965, Rollo's term of office ran out that November. Like that of Grieve, his appointment was not renewed by the new Conservative administration. Responsibility for industrial affairs was taken over by Alexander Forsyth, the newly appointed businessman whose career had been in chemicals. Thus within a few months the board had not only changed its industrial policy fundamentally but had also put its implementation into fresh hands. True to his word Skewis went out to sell the product as hard as he could. His sales drive was no different from those being pursued by other areas and other agencies. The techniques were those of the advertising agency- brochures, coupon advertising, films, press tours, exhibitions.

But the results were indifferent and proved no more successful than the pedestrian, less public methods employed previously. Indeed, because of the nature of its approach its failures tended to be more spectacular. Skewis did not stay long in his new post, leaving the board to seek his fortune with private enterprise in 1972. But in that relatively brief period—his public pyrotechnics aside—he laid the ground for some good work to be done.

It was a clear gain to the board's efforts to bring all the aspects of support to industry within one unit. Promotion, financial and personnel advice, marketing, factory construction and transport services, previously the responsibility of different sections of the board's structure, now could be welded together to present a more formidable and effective prospectus to the potential developer.

Of course there were weaknesses. Priority was given to advertising and promotion at one end and to finance at the other; what was missing was the hard know-how and control which would have come from men who had practical experience of industry. In the new set-up only one had that kind of background. The board chose as the successor to Skewis their chief economist Keith Farquharson. He had joined the organisation in 1968 after working in the oil industry and was much less convinced than his predecessor of the dividends to be obtained from regular and expensive exposure in the press. He adopted an approach which lay mid-way between the two extremes through which the board already had passed.

By this time oil was more than a smudge on the horizon. In the annual report for 1971, Andrew Gilchrist had written; 'The truth is that up to the end of 1971 none of the oil-related firms had laid a brick or hired a man in the Highland area. The impact of oil begins this year, 1972. . . .'[6] Much of that impact, it was realised, would stem from developments over which the board would have little influence because, first, they would result from national priorities and second, the finance required would be far in excess of the board's total yearly budget. The board saw as its main role the encouragement of non-oil enterprises which, in part, would counterbalance the explosion which the arrival of oil would cause and the minimising of the social and economic distortions which could be the outcome of the oil industry's massive investment onshore.

Partly because of that and partly in response to pressure from within the Highlands and islands the board began to devote more effort to cultivating its own backyard. In 1971 it designed a promotion campaign aimed at those already living and working in the area but more lasting dividends were expected from the decision to build up a network of local offices. Earlier experience in Shetland—where the board had been represented on the ground by a small staff since 1968 because of the difficulties imposed by the sheer distance between Inverness and Lerwick—gave the board confidence that getting closer to its customers was no bad thing.

Another out-station was added in Stornoway to serve the Western Isles and by 1980 the board also had staff in Wick and Lochgilphead and on Mull. Given that throughout this period the board was working under severe restrictions on staff recruitment imposed by the Scottish Office, this was a considerable achievement. It was reinforced by an initiative taken shortly after the arrival of Ken Alexander as chairman in 1976. This sprang from reports in the *West Highland Free Press* extolling the advantages of the multi-purpose cooperatives as developed in Eire. Written by Brian Wilson these reports suggested that the cooperatives would be worthy at least of examination by the board.[7]

Alexander accepted the idea and, along with the board's secretary visited Eire that summer. Like Wilson he was impressed by what he saw. Unlike the typical Scottish cooperative, which brought together a group of people, like farmers or fishermen, who were involved in a single activity, the Irish version brought together the community to invest in a range of enterprises. Further exchanges between Inverness and Dublin followed as staff were set to work to see if the idea could be transplanted successfully to the Highlands of Scotland. A visit to the Western Isles by representatives of Gaeltarra Eireann in the spring of 1977 prompted such a positive response from the islanders that the board devised a scheme which was launched the following November.

Initially the board confined the experiment to the Western Isles but hoped that the scheme could be extended further afield at a later date. To secure the active help of the board, communities had to set up steering committees which then had to devise 'sound programmes of action' as well as begin to raise local finance. If these conditions were met the board undertook to match local shares pound for pound, to provide a grant towards the salary of a manager and to use the board's normal grants and loans scheme to support projects devised by the cooperative.

To back its proposals the board appointed two field officers to advise local groups and published a guide book in Gaelic and English.[8] The response was speedy and by the end of the year six steering groups had been established in the islands. By 1980 Alexander was able to claim the board were confident of the scheme because of 'the impressive response by local communities who have already raised nearly £100,000'.[9] The board extended the scheme for a further three years, reporting that 34 activities with 22 full time, 61 part time and 13 seasonal employees were generating an annual community cooperative turnover of some £500,000. Ten community cooperatives had been registered, seven were operational and the scheme had broken out of its original geographic limits with one cooperative in Orkney at Papa Westray and another on the West Highland mainland at Acharacle.

During this period the board also set out on another fresh course in the pursuit of manufacturing industry. Like the cooperative scheme this, too, involved looking overseas. On this occasion, however, bigger fish were in prospect, prompting an expensive Concorde flight to New York by Alexander and the board secretary which enabled them to have a week-end break before they started a round of visits which began in Canada and went on to Iceland before they returned to the UK. Out of their visit came the proposal that the board should hire Venture Founders Corporation of Boston to seek out, assess and prepare for its consideration businesses of promise. The idea was worked on in what amounted to considerable secrecy so that Alexander's deputy, David Dunbar-Nasmith, who was responsible for industrial promotion, knew nothing of it until it arrived on his desk, fully worked out in a paper, within a few days of the board meeting which was to discuss it.

The idea, consequently, was not swallowed hook, line and sinker. Reservations were expressed at the meeting and doubts were voiced about how the board's own staff would react. It took a whole year, and further visits to New York and return journeys by VF's principals to the Highlands, before these doubts were stilled. What eventually emerged was Highland Venture Capital, a consortium of the board, the Bank of Scotland and the Industrial and Commercial Finance Corporation. The purpose of the consortium was to invest, by means of a risk capital fund, in businesses which were capable of growing into multi-million pound enterprises.[10] These, of course, were to be identified by Venture Founders Corporation for a fee in excess of £150,000.

Between £25,000 and £300,000 was to be invested as equity in each of the new businesses which would be run by entrepreneurs judged as capable of developing substantial firms in the Highlands and Islands by the mid-'eighties.

Venture Founders used methods which, at least in their initial phase, were not novel. These consisted of engineering as much publicity as possible about their existence and their purpose. Out of that they hoped to secure interest from around 250 potential businessmen. It was after that had been achieved that the novelty of their approach would appear.

Intensive screening would reduce that mass to between 16 and 20 entrepreneurs of real promise. This relatively small number then would experience a workshop which simulated the start-up of a new business. The workshop was planned to extend over three weekends, thus giving them six 16-hour days in which to demonstrate their strengths and weaknesses. Most of them, of course, would fall by the wayside, leaving VF with two to four people who, in their estimation, were committed totally to a project which, with the benefit of VF's advice and expertise, had a real chance of taking off.

From the board's point of view the scheme had obvious attractions. For a start it would conserve their own staff resources which remained under pressure. It also would sift out projects in a new way and construct them on a basis which, theoretically at least, would minimise the board's risk. Not everyone saw it that way, of course. Some officials thought that, in going outside, the board were undermining the role of their own staff. There would be no need, they argued, for an industrial division at all if the VF approach worked, an argument which might not be lost on Scottish Ministers anxious to reduce the role of the public sector.

The board accepted Ken Alexander's view that any new approach was worth trying. Accordingly, the contract was concluded and a public relations consultancy hired to organise the launch of the project. This took place on 14 January 1981 and was achieved by means of press conferences in Inverness and Glasgow, backed by radio and television interviews. The story which was revealed was that the board, the Industrial and Commercial Finance Corporation and the Bank of Scotland had come together to create a venture capital fund which would invest in new companies capable of growing into multi-million pound enterprises in the Highlands by the mid-'eighties. Offices had been set up in Edinburgh and

Glasgow as well as Inverness, and Venture Founders had been contracted to find and develop potential projects for the fund to consider.

Claiming that there were offices in Scotland's two chief cities was something of an exaggeration. What were there were two telephones which, if used by callers, would be answered by staff either of the bank, in Edinburgh, or of the Highland Fund in Glasgow who would refer the caller to the number of the office in Inverness. This one was genuine enough, being serviced by the board and manned by Joe Frye, one of the principals of Venture Founders. The board also assigned two of their staff to the project on the understanding that they would acquire some of the Americans' know-how and techniques.

The contract covered one 'cycle' of publicity, screening the initial response, carrying out one workshop and bringing between two and four potential projects to the fund for consideration. That meant securing upwards of 150 initial inquiries. To help attain that, VF secured access to those hopeful entrepreneurs who entered a competition run by the Scottish Council (Development and Industry) and aimed at uncovering new investment opportunities. The board also helped by encouraging staff to use its extensive contacts.

At the beginning of February Joe Frye reported, 'Since the scheme was launched we have dealt with 82 approaches, of which 60 are from the Highlands and islands. . . . There is no shortage of enterprise in the Highlands and the current recession does not seem to be dampening enthusiasm for new development or the expansion of existing businesses.'[11]

Almost ten months later, on 2 December, the first fruit of this endeavour was revealed.[12] At an exhibition in London the board announced that the fund was to invest £75,000 in acquiring 35 per cent of the share capital of Caiman of Caithness Ltd and that the board itself was to provide a further £75,000 of assistance, by way of grant and loan, to the project. Caiman had been in the pet food business since 1977, running a knackery which had moved from making a loss of over £3000 in its first year to recording a profit of the same magnitude on sales of more than £113,000 in 1980. The company's intention was to expand into the provision of meat for the human market and it expected this growth to create initially 20 new jobs. The board already had provided finance for the original scheme and its staff had worked with the firm since 1977.

According to Joe Frye, Caiman's principal 'revealed sound entrepreneurial abilities' and 'by the end of the workshops had emerged as one of four to six participants considered to have sufficient potential to justify entering the business planning phase of the programme'. David Dunbar-

Nasmith, the board's chairman, welcomed the project which would 'help realise our aim of encouraging a greater degree of livestock fattening and slaughtering in Caithness, and of developing more value-adding processes to utilise and market Caithness meat products'.

Crafts

The Irish Minister, Tom O'Donnell, during his visit to the Highlands in 1973 was impressed with the work done by the board to encourage the development of crafts. This had started very early in the board's life. Indeed one of the first projects it financed was a pottery. The region itself had attractions for craftsmen. The environment was congenial to their skills, a circumstance which, through its drawing of tourists, also created a basic market for their products. It was an advantage which almost demanded exploitation by the board.

In 1969 staff carried out a survey which suggested that the trade's annual turnover was around £500,000 and was capable of at least being doubled. On that evidence the board noted in its report that it was 'convinced that, properly organised, (the craft business) can tap new markets at home and abroad and reach a new peak of prosperity'.[13] Within a year the board had completed a further study which concentrated on the gifts bought by visitors. Not surprisingly it confirmed observation that holidaymakers purchased more than one item and had a strong preference for goods which actually were made in the Highlands and islands. In an effort to improve the marketing of such goods a symbol, Craftmade, was introduced as a mark guaranteeing the geographic authenticity of products. By the end of 1971, the mark was in use in 170 craft retail outlets.

That year also saw the birth of the Highlands and Islands Trade Fair. Held in November at Aviemore the fair was devised as a platform from which producers in the Highlands could sell direct to wholesalers from around the world. Its impact was immediate and widespread. Though criticisms were made of the poor quality of some of the products—the board was reluctant to set itself up as a judge of aesthetics—and of the interlopers from outside the region who were allowed space at the exhibition, its benefits were worthwhile. As it grew over the years, the fair brought the international market to the Highland producer's doorstep. It kept him abreast of changes in taste and demand and represented an opportunity for orders which craftsmen were reluctant to miss.

The board reinforced the success of the fair by taking individual companies to other trade exhibitions, both at home and overseas. Yet it constantly faced a dilemma which it has never been able to resolve. Its interests were in encouraging craftsmen to grow, to expand their markets, to occupy bigger premises and take on more workers. For many craftsmen such a programme was anathema. Their interests were in their own skills and in developing their individual potential. Though this was frequent cause of tension the board continued its constant flow of help and advice, whether the recipient was willing to expand or not. It accepted the reality that many communities could attract no productive enterprise but that of a craftsman.

In the early 'seventies it toyed with the idea of establishing a crafts centre in the Highlands which would offer training as well as marketing advice and attempt to improve standards of quality and design. In 1975 it commissioned a study of the possibilities. A year later the report recommended the building of such a centre, advocating 'an integrated approach to the development of the craft industry, including advice and practical help in the fields of marketing, information and design together with a range of training functions with the emphasis on itinerant services'.[14] A small steering committee, including representatives of craft and government interests from outside the Highlands was set up to refine these proposals.

The board's view was that 'the essential justification for a centre of the kind proposed lies in the contribution which it could make to the future development of the economy of the Highlands and islands, and indeed of the national economy. . . . Our experience . . . has amply demonstrated the industry's potential for growth . . . it is estimated that total sales of Highland craft products (excluding Shetland knitwear and Harris tweed) rose from £350,000 in 1968 to £3.5 million in 1975.'[15]

Much of that increase, it is clear, could be accounted for by the rapid increase in the rate of inflation during these years but there can be little argument that the bigger proportion of it had been caused by the board's efforts. In 1973 it had strengthened these further by breathing new life into a training scheme which had been begun by the Crofters' Commission six years earlier. The heart of the plan was to provide advice and financial assistance to individuals living in crofting communities so that they could take special training courses in craft and other skills. It was a cheap method of building up a community's skills as well as extending an individual's opportunities. In 1976 alone, forty-four people completed courses at a total cost of around £2000 to the board.[16]

New ventures were set up at a steady rate. In 1974 financial assistance was given to twenty; in 1976 the number receiving grant or loan help was ten, including a jewellery design and manufacturing business in Argyll and several of the, by then inevitable potteries. All of this gave the board a strong hand in the negotiations about the proposed craft centre. These were concluded in 1977 when a formal proposal was submitted to the Secretary of State who eventually gave his approval in the late summer of 1978. The centre was to be known as Highland Craftpoint, with about two thirds of its capital and operating costs coming from the board and the remainder from the Scottish Development Agency. Its essential purpose, the board explained, was 'to stimulate further commercial development in the field of craft production'.[17] It would employ eighteen at the outset and offer training, technical and information services, design help, research and development and marketing.

Within the board an argument, which touched upon its fundamental approach to its work, raged for months over the centre's location. Alexander took the view that Craftpoint had to be built close to an airport, close to the A9 and within easy distance of Inverness. His case was that such a central location was vital to the proper functioning of the development which had to enjoy ease of access from all parts of the Highlands and islands as well as from outside the region. Others argued that Craftpoint should be seen as a unique opportunity for the board to back all it had said, and continued to say, about the need to secure projects for the more remote parts of the region. This was an occasion when the board actually had the choice of location within its own grasp. If it placed the new complex in the east it would be carrying out an action and for reasons which it had deplored often enough when they applied to a private development.

Over the course of several meetings the opposing cases were tested, with Bobby Fasken eventually putting a strong plea for the board to decide in favour of building Craftpoint in Caithness which, though still on the east coast, was in need of new investment and was, on some definitions, a difficult area. It was certainly a 'remote' area.

But Alexander prevailed. The spot finally chosen was Beauly, about fifteen miles north of Inverness on the A9 and in the most populous and favoured part of the Highlands. Site work began in the later part of 1979. Staff were employed before the end of the following year and Craftpoint began its first training programmes in the Spring of 1981. On 10 July it was opened formally by Her Majesty the Queen.

Moray Firth Development

During the early years of the board the initials MFD (Moray Firth Development) came to signal not only the height of its ambitions but also the pitfalls
into which these ambitions could disappear.

If anything could be said to provide the key to the board's approach to
industrial development at that time then MFD was it. Grieve and his team
were after big fish and the area around the Moray and Cromarty Firths was
clearly the biggest bait they could design. The area had many advantages.
Its abundance of historic and pre-historic sites, Grieve was fond of claiming,
demonstrated that even our remote ancestors had found these attractions
irresistible. Its geography, its geology, its topography and its climate were
assets which, now in the second half of the twentieth century, ought to be
attractive to major investors.

At the end of February 1967 Grieve outlined the approach at some length
in a speech to the Inverness Chamber of Commerce. In promoting MFD, he
told the Highland capital's businessmen, the board hoped to benefit the
whole Highland area and the whole economy of the UK. He went on:

The latter will be helped by attracting industries which, as in the case of whisky and Harris
tweed, will largely be export-orientated and thus contribute to the balance of payments. In
addition the sizeable expansion of population here will contribute to the national objectives
of relieving congestion in the south and moving the UK centre of gravity northwards.
Within the Highlands the plan aims to establish a major centre of modern job opportunity
for those within and indeed without the Highlands, offering a wide range of jobs and
conditions in all respects 'comparable with the best now available in the UK and including
opportunities for those with higher technical or university training;

to establish a major centre which can offer within the region the range of commercial,
social, cultural and other activities which, together with the job opportunity I have already
mentioned, form the matrix of attraction of a modern city;

to act as a counter to the emigration of Highlanders and islanders who at present have to
move away to obtain suitable jobs;

to demonstrate to those in the south that enterprises founded in the Highlands are capable
of thoroughly profitable operation without recourse to revenue subsidy;

to offer a home market of reasonable size for the region's products, such as food, which will
strengthen the position of the primary producers of the area and give a sounder base for
adding value locally to their products. It will also require, and provide a basis of demand for,
improvements in transport and other social provisions as well as benefiting from,
improvements in recreation and tourist provision;

to help balance the economic structure of the region in which the distinctive feature is the
very small representation of manufacturing industry and to improve considerably the net
regional product.

Figure 6. Spinning shed, MacLeod's mill, Shawbost

Figure 7. MacLeod's mill, Shawbost

By the time Grieve made that speech the board had made its ambitions clear—and the opposition to these would ultimately bring the board to its knees. At issue was Invergordon Chemical Enterprises and its creator Frank Thomson.

The Secretary of State had appointed Thomson as a member of the board to replace Willie Logan, his original choice of Highland industrialist, who had been killed in an air crash. On taking up his part-time post Thomson, who ran Invergordon Distillery, had made no secret of his hope of establishing a petro-chemical complex on the Cromarty Firth. His scheme obtained the support of Product Planning—not surprising because they had constructed the initial proposal in a study commissioned by Thomson as managing director of Invergordon Distillery—which had been asked by the board to undertake a credibility study of major industrial development around the shores of the Moray Firth. Their report, completed in August 1966, concluded that such investment was possible and could be based on Thomson's proposed complex as well as on cheap power which would attract companies in mineral processing and food processing.

To outsiders it seemed as if the board's ambitions knew no bounds. Along with Ross and Cromarty County Council it appointed the Jack Holmes Planning Group to produce a regional plan for the whole MFD area predicated on a growth of population to around 250,000 in ten to fifteen years. Speaking of the idea Grieve referred to industries, docks, labour and housing having to be considered and developed along parallel lines. The ICE project was estimated to cost around £50 million and its first phase alone would require 300 acres.

But for some time a part-time employee of the board, Philip Durham, concerned with the way things were being done, had been using confidential information from the board's records in an attempt to undermine the entire effort. He concentrated his attack on the fact that the board had given financial assistance to schemes with which its members, particularly Thomson, were associated. Despite a great deal of effort no one seemed prepared to listen to his case until, in the week Grieve spoke to the local chamber of commerce, the board learned that the Sunday Express was ready to publish material based on Durham's dossier.

Grieve had outlined the ambitious MFD strategy on Tuesday 28 February. Three days later the board's assistant secretary made a night journey to Kildary in Ross-shire to deliver a dismissal notice into the Durham's hands. The Sunday Express published on 5 March. That afternoon, in the absence of the chairman and his deputy, two members of the board, John Robertson and Prophet Smith called a press conference in an effort to put out the fire. But they succeeded only in kindling a blaze that spread, eventually forcing the Secretary of State to make two statements in the House.

In conjunction with the second on 23 March, Thomson resigned. Clearly feeling he was the victim of a deliberate campaign, he told the press: 'We who truly love the Highlands have lived through a dark period of anguish, despair and misery these last few weeks. We must set aside these feelings and all of us, Gaelic and English-speaking, bind ourselves together in a united force to make the Highlands the place we want it to be—where our children can live in social significance and economic parity with those who live in other parts of Britain.'[18]

But Thomson was not the only one to be emotional. According to *The Scotsman*, the Secretary of State's statement was 'the most difficult of his career'. Sometimes, its political correspondent recorded, '(his) voice faltered with emotion, sometimes he stumbled over words as he read from his carefully prepared brief'.[19] Faced with an Opposition thirsting for his blood, he yet managed to give the board and Thomson a clean bill of health. There had been no impropriety.

At least one of his Cabinet colleagues admired his skill. In his diaries Richard Crossman recorded, 'The affair smelt badly and looking at the statement before it was made I thought he wouldn't get away with it. But he did. There was no row and no sensation. I reflected that he showed considerable skill. . . .'[20]

Thomson claimed privately that what he saw as an orchestrated campaign against him had played into the hands of the major petroleum companies like BP, Shell and Esso. They, he claimed, had not relished the thought of competition, particularly when that was to come from a source partly owned by an American company, Occidental Petroleum. Occidental clearly felt that they had been let down by Willie Ross and his Scottish Office team, especially over the question of Thomson's resignation. Yet they made no immediate announcement of their intention to turn their backs on Invergordon. Indeed almost a year later Grieve told reporters[21] that he did not know whether or not Occidental remained interested in the project. But abandon the Cromarty Firth the company did.

The board was severely shaken by the whole experience. Bob Grieve confessed he had considered resignation but had decided that such an action would weaken the board beyond redemption. It was only later that he could look back and claim that, through those spring months of 1967, the entire organisation had been tempered by fire. More immediately he was unable to keep Robertson, who all through had been one of the chief exponents of MFD on the board, from criticising the Scottish Ministers and the Scottish Office staff. On 7 July Robertson resigned following a meeting between the board and the Secretary of State.

In a letter to the Secretary of State Robertson made it clear that his action was a protest at the attitude of the Scottish Office to Highland development. He wrote:

When you were good enough to ask me to join the Highlands and Islands Development Board, I wrote to you outlining my views on how Highland development must go. In particular I said I firmly believed that big enterprises, and a willingness to do things differently from heretofore, were keys to *solving* the problem. I added that my understanding of your intentions for the board was such that you would not want someone holding these view on it, but that if they were acceptable to you I should be happy to serve.

Since then I have been concerned, among other things, with big enterprises in connection with Moray Firth Development and I have been increasingly dismayed by the attitude of the Scottish Office. This has been communicated both to you and to your senior officials.

It has become clear from our work that the problem is quite soluble over all our area, covering half of Scotland, *given* the will to solve it and willingness to deploy the necessary resources. I see no sign whatever of the requisite will to *solve* the problem on the part of the Scottish Office and, of course, in terms of the Act, this is crucial. The attitude to proposals of real substance is uniformly a negative search for the maximum of difficulty. To this is added a degree of indecision and confusion which is quite startling. The board have emphasised that we do not stand in a static situation and that delay or indecision are just as effective in driving away potential development as a straight 'no'.

Turning to Moray Firth Development, and setting aside entirely the 'petro-chemical complex' and the induced controversy surrounding it, the position is that you have before you two major submissions from the board and definitive major proposals from commercial interests of the very highest repute and standing made jointly to us and the Board of Trade. I say confidently that when these proposals can be made public it will be apparent to all that not only are they excellent for Highland development but also excellent for the UK in general and the balance of payments in particular. Your reply contained only a peremptory instruction to do nothing whatever about them and to have no contact with the firms concerned.

This is characteristic of all our contacts with your departments on major proposals which involve using methods novel to the UK but which have proved successful in the hands of several development agencies similar to our board in other parts of the world. The board would be very glad to engage in constructive discussions with the aim of overcoming the real problems posed, for example, by financial stringency but unfortunately the only reaction is a series of alarmed objections on the line 'it's different, don't do it'.

Again leaving aside the 'petro-chemical complex' the position is that you have been specifically asked whether any progress can be made on the major submissions from the board and commercial companies on industrial developments or in the matter of natural resource exploration. The replies have been so indecisive and such delay has been incurred as to produce a worse result than a straight 'no' would have done.

Merely to illustrate that this negative attitude is not confined to the Moray Firth, I would mention also a major land project in the Western Isles whose future is being prejudiced by a quite gratuitous difficulty introduced by the Scottish Office. Here again we have no signs of advance.

It was a lengthy letter but it touched on the main issues which were exacerbating the board's relationship with those civil servants through whom it reported to and, in theory at least, was controlled by, the Secretary of State. The Secretary of State denied that there was a rift. 'The Government are not opposed to Moray Firth development,' he told a press conference at which he announced Robertson's resignation, 'and it is nonsense to suggest that there is opposition in the Scottish Office.' Anxious to cool tempers he added, 'I hope I can take some of the heat out of this controversy, which has been based on speculation and certainly not on material substance.'[22]

Grieve was not so sure. In the work of any development agency, he suggested there were criticisms about the control of civil servants. These might be justified to a greater or lesser degree. 'It is up to the Government and the board to have their fight out on this issue,' he said. 'We are doing this. So far as I am concerned, it has come to nothing like the intolerable stage.'[23]

Ministers and officials at Scottish Office were embarrassed by the sweep and scope of the board's approach. Here was their creature—at that time the board could not offer financial assistance in excess of £25,000 to any project without their blessing—talking of the need for special deals on energy prices to encourage power-intensive industries, even, perhaps, a new power station in the Moray Firth area, £50 million petro-chemical complexes, downstream activities and new urban development. Undoubtedly it was a shock to their systems.

That they intended the board to confine its ambitions to small projects was no secret. Dr Dickson Mabon, Ross's Minister of State, made that clear enough a month later when he said, 'The board was never established to set up multi-million pound enterprises. It does not have the money or the expertise.'[24] He spoke when Grieve was attending an international conference in Berlin. Board staff took the opportunity to respond by sending their chairman a telegram which said simply, 'Continue to think big.' To Grieve that at least was vital; securing a major development would be the key psychological breakthrough for Highland development as well as the restorer of the board's leaking credibility. He did not have long to wait.

On 4 October in the course of his address to the Labour Party Conference at Scarborough, Harold Wilson announced the Governement's intention to encourage the building of two aluminium smelters. 'We are prepared,' he told delegates, 'to build publicly owned power stations to work in partnership with private enterprise smelting industries, the electricity to be supplied at a price based on the station's generating costs.'[25] The Government, it seemed, was inviting the aluminium companies to discuss the terms of special contracts with the electricity boards and to put forward to Ministers specific proposals for setting up smelting plants in development areas.

To the board it was a case of apparently having their old clothes stolen. Wilson's initiative contained two elements of their case for MFD—the provision of cheap power and the aluminium reduction plant. In any race for the Government's new project the Moray Firth area, and Invergordon in particular, had a head start.

Alcan already had had talks with the board and had expressed an interest in the Cromarty Firth site. As one of the contenders, the company took part in a meeting at St Andrew's House the day after Wilson's speech with representatives of the Scottish Office, the North of Scotland Hydro Electric Board and the HIDB.[26]

Alcan did not have the field to itself. Another five major concerns, including RTZ and British Aluminium responded to the Government's challenge. The attractions of Invergordon were confirmed in October when senior executives of BA visited the area. Early the following month both BA and Alcan sought planning permission.

Although doubts were expressed elsewhere about the strength of the Scottish case for one of the smelters—the Government envisaged one coming on stream in 1970, the second in 1974—the board was confident that the Highlands was about to land the big fish it had been seeking. Eventually three plants were given the Government's blessing—BA at Invergordon, Alcan in Northumberland and RTZ in Anglesey. BA's deal on power with the NSHEB was based on the costs of generation at the new nuclear station, Hunterston B, the contracts for which had been placed only in October.

The Government's decision on Invergordon was announced by the President of the Board of Trade, Anthony Crosland, to the House of Commons on 24 July 1968. The months since Wilson's Scarborough declaration had been hectic but fruitful.

In the early stages of the campaign for the smelter, a public inquiry had taken place at Dingwall into Ross and Cromarty's proposal to rezone agricultural land at Invergordon for industrial purposes. Before the reporter's findings found their way to the Secretary of State's desk, the Holmes Group's study and recommendations were given to the board.[27] Ross gave his approval to the county council's plans on 7 June. Eleven days later the board published the Holmes report at a press conference taken by Mabon. Although the subject of a sour 'dreams for sale'[28] comment by the *Inverness Courier*, the group's recommendations were welcomed by the authorities which would have to contend with the implications of the smelter's arrival. Murdo Nicholson, convener of the Ross and Cromarty County Council, saw them as 'challenging and provocative'.[29] The report could not have been better timed. By defining the problems and the opportunities presented by major development around the Moray Firth it gave the local authorities and others concerned a basis on which to work. In September the Scottish Office set up a special working party, including representatives of Ross and Cromarty, Inverness-shire, the board and British Aluminium to oversee the task of assimilating the £37 million plant into the community.

Meanwhile Grieve was overjoyed at the outcome of the board's campaign. He commented after Crosland's announcement: 'When you get an undertaking of this size coming to the Highlands, so decisively bringing the whole centre of gravity further north, there are no criticisms, no disappointment, only thankfulness. It ought to be regarded by everyone as a superb prize.'[30]

The petro-chemical prize continued to remain elusive, even though the whole idea had been revived in the spring with the entrance of Eoin Mekie and Grampian Chemicals. His £55 million scheme provoked a great deal of scepticism and from the beginning Grieve, a little wiser now, attempted to make the board's role in the matter absolutely clear. The board welcomed the proposal, he had told the press conference which Mekie summoned in March 1968 to explain his plans. But he added, 'There is a point that the Highland Board can take a thing to and after that the whole question of its economic feasibility in the national economy is handled by the Government. The initial stages have been reached. Mr Mekie from now onwards has got to take this to the stage where it can be approved by the Government or a judgment is made by them.'[31]

Despite Mekie's clever—some thought unprincipled—public relations (his company hired a bulldozer for a day to provide proof of work beginning at the site) his project never got off the drawing board. Indeed that was to remain the fate of the idea throughout the following decade. Despite support from Ross, who twice upset the findings of public inquiries to approve the re-zoning of the land necessary, and despite the intervention of major world-wide interests, the complex which had inspired the board from the beginning was still an idea on the drawing board as the 1980s began.

Yet Grieve's basic case that the Moray Firth area was ideal for major development was amply demonstrated. As the international oil industry exploited the resources of the North Sea its suppliers made massive investments in two platform construction yards and a pipe coating plant on the shores of the firth.

Small Firms

MFD and petro-chemical complexes may have captured the headlines throughout the seventies but the board also maintained a steady flow of investment into small manufacturing enterprises. In 1970 it placed nearly £¾ million of grants and loans with 60 such companies which were expected to create nearly 850 jobs; in 1975 over £1 million went to 50 who intended employing 425; and in 1980 £1.3 million was invested in 58 who estimated their employment requirements at just under 300. At the same time it carried out an ambitious factory building effort. It submitted its first programme to the Secretary of State in 1970, a year in which it received approval to acquire sites at Inverness, Muir of Ord and in Shetland and also completed its first bespoke factory at Dalcross Airport. By 1980 it had over 80 industrial properties throughout the Highlands and islands and was planning to embark on a new programme which, valued at £3 million, would add another 39 to that stock.

By and large its work with small firms was successful. Though there were failures the board's bad debt provision in 1980 amounted to 4.3 per cent of the £18.1 million balance of loans then outstanding. By 1980, of course, it was politically advantageous to help small businesses since that was a distinct policy aim of the new Conservative Government. But it required no change in the board's approach. The board had been encouraging companies in the textile trade, electronics industry, food processing, engineering, printing and, indeed, in most kinds of manufacturing and processing that conceivably could strengthen the regional economy.

The board also devoted resources to aiding existing firms. This was particularly so on the islands. For obvious reasons, they did not have the kind of locations that footloose entrepreneurs considered as offering them the best prospects—though there were exceptions like knitwear, the products of which gained some *cachet* from being made in an island environment. On Lewis and Harris the board's energies were directed through the early and mid-seventies towards the Harris Tweed industry. Uniquely Hebridean and, because of its nature, ideally suited to the crofting community, the industry for years had underpinned the island economy. But by 1970 it was suffering a slump of historic proportions.

In the next year the board, following the completion of a special study, began to argue that what Harris Tweed required was a new marketing

Figure 8. Weaving Harris Tweed, Carloway

approach. That, in turn, depended on new designs which would be impossible unless the industry replaced its traditional single width with double width cloth. To get to that point, of course, required the manufacture of a loom capable of weaving a double width. A prototype was commissioned. The manufacturers in England found it relatively easy to make the loom but the nut they could not crack was making one that the weaver could power, as he did his existing machine, by pedalling. In its 1973 report the board noted, 'It is hoped that further modifications will shortly produce a loom which will produce cloth at an acceptable rate and with a tolerable level of physical effort.'[32] But pedal power was a fading option, with the weaver's muscles being replaced by an electric motor. A year later the board reported, 'Studies of the comparative operating economics of manual and power looms indicated that there would be a strong case on economic grounds for introducing the use of power concurrently with the introduction of double width weaving.'[33]

Though this was no small matter the board claimed that 'sentiment within all segments of the industry had moved overwhelmingly in favour of the use of power'. The Harris Tweed Association, the marketing arm of the trade, was to open talks with the Department of Trade to explore the possibility of varying the definition of Harris tweed and the conditions governing the use of the Orb trade mark. At the same time a committee, with representatives of the board, HTA, the Hebridean Spinners Advisory Committee, small producers and the Transport and General Workers' Union, was set up 'to supervise and co-ordinate the complex preparatory work needed to pave the way for the introduction of a power driven double width loom'.

The board's plans included providing finance to help weavers obtain the new looms as well as building small factories at several locations to house the new machinery. In practice it was threatening not only to change the industry but also to alter the crofter-weaver's way of life. His independence, supported by his own weaving shed near the croft house, would be weakened if he were to accept double width cloth and all its implications. Over that ground a battle erupted. The *West Highland Free Press*, in particular, campaigned vigorously against the proposals, James Grant, chairman of the HTA and a part-time member of the board, seemed sadly out of touch with opinion among the weavers as he argued for the double width proposals.

The intensity of the opposition provoked some hesitation. The association decided not to apply to the Department of Trade for an amendment to the regulations controlling the Orb trade mark until, despite what the board had said in 1974, it 'was satisfied that a consensus of opinion in favour of the proposals exists throughout the industry.'[34]

Any hope of a consensus disappeared in the spring of 1976 when in a heavy poll the weavers overwhelmingly rejected the board's package. Ironically, recording the end of its effort in its report, the board also conceded that, thanks to the vagaries of the fashion market, demand for the traditional product of the industry was on the way up again.[35]

Notes

1   HIDB, First Report, 1965–6, p 4
2   Central Scotland, a programme for development and growth; Cmnd 2188; November 1963 (HMSO)
3   *The Scotsman* 7 February 1965
4   *Sruth* 3 March 1969
5   *Sruth* 30 April 1970
6   HIDB, Sixth Report, 1971 p 5
7   *West Highland Free Press* 2 July 1976
8   Community Cooperatives, a guide, HIDB, 1977
9   *North* 7 July/August 1980, HIDB
10 Press release issued by Highland Venture Capital, 14 January 1981
11 Press release issued for Highland Venture Capital by HIDB, 2 February 1981
12 Press release 49/81, 2 December 1981, HIDB
13 HIDB, Fourth Report, 1969, p 24
14 HIDB, Eleventh Report, 1976, p 44
15 Ibid. p 46
16 Ibid. p 56
17 HIDB, Thirteenth Report, 1978, p 39
18 *The Scotsman* 24 March 1967
19 *The Scotsman* 24 March 1967
20 *The Diaries of a Cabinet Minister*, vol. 2, 1966–8, Richard Crossman (Hamish Hamilton/Jonathan Cape, 1977), p 290
21 *The Scotsman* 31 July 1968
22 *The Scotsman* 8 July 1967
23 *The Scotsman* 8 July 1967
24 *The Scotsman* 31 August 1967: Dr Mabon's remarks at an Edinburgh University summer school caused a minor political storm, Russell Johnston arguing that they were evidence that ministers were trying to downgrade the board and its work
25 A full account of the Government's role in the creation of the modern British aluminium smelting industry is given by Edmund Dell in his book *Political Responsibility and Industry* (George Allen and Unwin, 1973)

26   *The Scotsman* 6 October 1967
27   *Inverness Courier* 5 April 1968
28   *Inverness Courier* 18 June 1968
29   *Inverness Courier* 18 June 1968
30   *Inverness Courier* 26 July 1968
31   *Inverness Courier* 29 March 1968
32   HIDB, Eighth Report, 1973, p 41
33   HIDB, Ninth Report, 1974, p 47
34   HIDB, Tenth Report, 1975, p 42
35   HIDB, Eleventh Report, 1976, p 44

LAND

Much of the land could be better used. Highland and
national interest requires that it should be

To many, how the board tackled the problem of misuse of land would be its key test. There was an air of anticipation; at long last an alternative centre to the power of the landlords had been established. Backed by a sympathetic government and with access to finance, the board, it seemed, could not fail to redress the abuses suffered by Highlanders and islanders for two centuries.

Land, its ownership and its uses was an emotional issue buried within the community's spirit, a latent but potent part of the folk memory. The success of the 7:84 group's tour in the early seventies with *The Cheviot, the Stag and the Black, Black Oil* tapped that source. The drama's account of the people living at the mercy of economic and social forces beyond their control drew from that source among audiences in Scotland's urban heartland as well as in the village halls of Highland communities. Its force, and the intensity of the memory, were illustrated at the play's performance in Brora. One scene called for an actor to speak the words of Patrick Sellar, who secured his place in history by bringing improvements to the Sutherland Estates in an inhuman way. As the player addressed the audience in words that had been spoken 150 years before, an old lady in the front of the hall rose to her feet to harangue 'Sellar' in Gaelic.

Perhaps her greatgrandfather had been alive at the time of Sellar's trial[1] in Inverness on charges of arson and culpable homicide—of which he was acquitted—but his human guilt seemed as fresh in her mind as if he still were planning the clearance of Strathnaver from the comfort of the factor's office of Sutherland Estates.

Few issues have dominated a nation's history so much and for so long as the Highland Clearances. An economic response to the changing conditions of the late eighteenth and early nineteenth centuries, they yet can provoke passionate debate. No matter that much of the emigration from the Highlands and islands at that time took place on an organised basis, arranged and financed often by the land owners; no matter that the emigrants, in turn, dispossessed the Red Indian in North America; the clearances are still seen as a stain on Scotland's social history.

Much of that they owe to the behaviour of Patrick Sellar as he worked on behalf of the Countess of Sutherland and her husband, Lord Stafford. His actions in Strathnaver in 1814 'assumed the definitive aspects of a final solution'.[2] Cottages were put to the flame whether or not they had been evacuated by the elderly or cleared of livestock, a brutal approach which has echoed down the years as a running commentary on the land question.

Attempts had been made since the immediate aftermath of Culloden to encourage development. The Crown Commissioners appointed to look after the estates annexed from disaffected chiefs after the '45 took an interest in fishing and communications as well as in education and farming. The work of Thomas Telford in the early nineteenth century was in part a response to the tide of emigration from the Highlands while the first Crofters Commission, set up in 1886 following the report of the Napier Commission,[3] had powers to fix and revise rents, to rule on the compensation made to any one giving up a croft, to provide for the enlargement of crofts and to regulate the management of common rights in grazing, seaweed and peat. Before the century was out, the Congested Districts Board[4] had been given the duty of developing agriculture, fishing, creating new holdings and providing public works.

Yet the problem remained. Emigration continued to drain the area, each decennial census recording the steady erosion. Ownership of the land continued to be held by a few families and companies.[5]

The founders of the HIDB seemed clear that the two chief targets of their creation would be to reverse the drift of people away from the Highlands and to tackle the land issue. Speaking in the debate on the second reading in the House of Commons, of the Highlands and Islands Development (Scotland) Bill, Willie Ross, the Secretary of State, remarked, 'Land is the basic resource of the Highlands and any plan for economic and social development would be meaningless if proper use of land were not a part of it.'

Such ambition required them to give the board a parcel of special powers. This allowed the board to acquire land, compulsorily if necessary, and to hold, manage or dispose of land; others, such as its power to carry on businesses at its own hand and to give financial aid to development projects, though not specific to land, were relevant.

In setting out on its task on 1 November 1965, the board, in so far as land was concerned, had not only a great deal of practical experience, but also access to a substantial amount of ground work which already had been prepared. From 1946 to 1949 its chairman, Bob Grieve, had been regional planning officer for the Highlands in the Department of Health; Prophet Smith, a full-time member, had come from the headquarters of the Scottish Agricultural Organisation Society; and John Robertson, the youngest of Willie Ross's appointments, was a farmer in Easter Ross. The groundwork had been done by several organisations and most recently by the Advisory Panel on the Highlands and Islands which, the previous year, had produced a report on land use.[6]

Perhaps it was because of the experience of its members and because of the problems outlined by the panel that the board was hesitant initially in its approach to the question of land, whether in terms of assisting farming projects or in the more fundamental aspect of ownership. Certainly there were formidable reasons for a cautious approach. Above all others, the farming industry had its own institutional structure to serve its interests; it had its own Government department, jealous of its province; it had publicly funded research agencies working on its behalf; and, of course, its own scheme of financial aid from the taxpayer. Finding a useful, dynamic role within that established network, the board realised, was not going to be done quickly.

On ownership, the board also thought it ought to tread warily. The big estates in any event were suspicious, while those who would support the board if it made any attempt to demonstrate its compulsory powers would not forgive lightly an effort that misfired. At the end of 1966 the board had been in office for fourteen months. It had the outline of an administrative structure, begun to build a planning and research team, set the basis for a finance group, but had not appointed any staff with skills or experience relevant to its most intractable problem—land use.

Throughout these early months it had directed a great deal of energy to assessing the difficulty. It had close and continuing contact with the Department of Agriculture and Fisheries, it had met representatives of the National Farmers' Union, it had spoken to the Crofters Commission, as well as the Federation of Crofters Unions, it had exchanged views with the Scottish Landowners Federation and sought advice from the agricultural colleges and the Hill Farming Research Organisation.

That was a measure perhaps of how sensitive the board considered the issue. Committed to producing a land use plan for the Highlands and islands, the board proceeded slowly. Its first report[7] offered the reason that '. . . the preparation of such a plan is not a matter that can be hurried for land is not a resource with which it is proper to take quick decisions or in the use of which it is possible to make changes overnight'. At that stage it was able only to offer some tentative suggestions. Any plan had to stem from a policy; basic to that policy was the board's determination to see that the region produced as much as it could from the land; productivity and employment, therefore, were key elements.

In the opening chapter of that first report, entitled 'The Challenge', Bob Grieve wrote that agriculture had to remain an important part of the Highland economy. He went on, 'The board believes that much more can be produced from the Highlands but it is very clear that this is highly unlikely to be accompanied by an increasing population in these activities; rather is it likely to be accompanied by a drop because of more efficient and mechanised methods. The board will back any move in the direction of more production and where, as in certain highly productive enterprises, it means also more jobs the board will redouble its efforts to help. Here, therefore, the result would be more food from the Highlands for the rest of the country rather than more people for the Highlands.'

Significantly there was no mention of ownership, either in 'The Challenge', where the chairman was trying to set out a broad strategy, or in the section dealing with land. Which was not to say the issue had been forgotten. That was a luxury not allowed the board by the press or, indeed by its political supporters in the Labour Party—or for that matter by people with development ideas which were being hindered by uncooperative landlords.

A great deal of publicity that year had surrounded the case of the locked gates of Strathfarrar. One of the most scenic glens in the Eastern Highlands, Strathfarrar had had bestowed upon it the benefit of a macadammed road by the North of Scotland Hydro Electric Board[8] in the course of dam construction. The co-proprietor of the ground, Lord Lovat, had received substantial compensation for the disturbance of his fishing rights by the hydro scheme. No sooner had the work been completed, than the gate appeared at the foot of the glen closing off the public road. The key had to be requested from the occupier of a nearby house. To many this seemed a classic case of landlord obstructionism. Inevitably the board was drawn into the debate which raged in the press but confessed it could do little to open the gate. A suggestion that the cover of its first report to the Secretary of State should be a picture of the chained and padlocked gate was dismissed by Bob Grieve as being too provocative. Provocative or not, the issue was to feature prominently throughout the board's first fifteen years. It was to do so largely because of the behaviour of one landlord, Dr John Green, of Bexhill-on-Sea, Sussex. Even in the course of the board's first twelve months he had been suggested as an ideal target for the board's compulsory powers.

Figure 9. Raasay House, Raasay

Raasay lies along the north east flank of Skye, sheltering between it and mainland Applecross. It is the unlikely site of a row of miners' cottages which, though familiar in the Lothians and Lanarkshire, were built in this remote spot when the island's resources of iron ore were being plundered towards the end of the nineteenth century. A walker might cover the island in a day, certainly noting on his journey the dominant 1500-foot flat-topped Dun Caan, and perhaps the lushness of the Raasay's growth, especially around Inverarish, and Churchtown Bay.

Dr Green first ventured to Raasay from his comfortable retreat in the Home Counties in 1961 when he bought from the Secretary of State Raasay House Hotel which, in addition to thirty bedrooms and a magnificent library, also possessed nine acres of land and another building, Borrodale House. Appetite whetted, he went on to relieve the Department of Agriculture and Fisheries of its responsibilities for Raasay Home Farm and its 180 acres in 1962 and for a small two-roomed cottage. By 1966 his possessions seemed like a job lot—a walled orchard, a garden with greenhouses, kennels, a pier, a jetty and inner harbour and a loch. For all of this the sum he was due the Secretary of State was £7688, a sum which at that time he had not paid in full.[9]

He did not limit his deals to the Government. In 1962 he had bought privately another property with over 21 acres for £2250. In July 1966 Russell Johnston, Liberal MP for Inverness-shire, had brought Raasay—by then suffering from the neglect of its absentee owner—to the attention of the Scottish Office. George Willis, the Minister of State, had replied that the board were to be asked for their views on the economic situation and scope for development on the island.

The board, the Scottish Office, the politicians and the people of Raasay were setting out on a road that would have no end until 1979. As they journeyed along, it became clear that far from being the powerful body imagined by its makers the board suffered from a flaw in its make-up which had been present from the moment the Highlands and Islands (Scotland) Development Act had received the Royal Assent.

Grappling with the task of developing agriculture was not so strenuous. In the course of its second year, the board approved help to sixteen projects ranging from marketing of calves from the Uists to intensive pig production. The sum involved was over £117,000 and, though relatively small, it was a beginning. By October 1968 it was able to publish an Occasional Bulletin[10] outlining its attitude to agriculture. Underlying that approach, it said, was the undertaking it had given in its first report that it would 'back any move in the direction of more production' though it had acknowledged that 'the result would be more food from the Highlands for the rest of the country rather than more people for the Highlands'.

The bulletin accepted that the board had 'a clear responsibility to promote, encourage and assist the development of a healthy and prosperous agriculture within the Highlands and Islands' and that it believed 'that the level of agricultural production in its area can and should be increased, and that the productivity of land and labour can be raised by more efficient methods and the more intensive use of land'. The board hoped that the farming community would seek its financial help, especially in the form of capital loans which would encourage more intensive methods of production. It set out the criteria by which it would judge such applications: viability, employment, and assistance from other statutory sources such as DAFS and the Crofters Commission.

In cases where it agreed to provide finance the board promised to retain an interest through periodic reports on the projects concerned. More importantly the bulletin stated, 'The board will initiate agricultural development projects in particular geographical areas or commodity sectors. Where appropriate the board may implement such a project itself or seek to achieve that end in cooperation with one or more existing bodies with experience and responsibilities in the relevant field'. Further, it would prepare and/or have prepared 'draft plans for the comprehensive development of selected areas, will discuss these with interested persons and organisations and will help to establish a procedure for implementing approved proposals in a coordinated fashion'.

Heady stuff indeed, reflecting perhaps what the board saw as the political necessity of pushing ahead with the kind of work which had been foreshadowed by the Highland Panel. In particular it looked upon the Strath of Kildonan as an inheritance from the panel which, in its land use report, had said that the Strath merited attention. The board agreed, considering that Kildonan offered the opportunity and need for a comprehensive approach.

A great deal of work had been done. In agreement with the landowners the Forestry Commission had completed a plantability survey which, in 1965, reported that the Strath held 35,000 acres that were plantable. The proprietors accepted that, of the total, 5000 could be planted. By the time it published its bulletin in 1968 the board had built on that work. It had carried out extensive consultations with the landowners, DAFS and the Forestry Commission; on the basis of these talks, the commission's survey of the six estates in the Strath, an examination by DAFS of the area's 'optimum capacity for agriculture' and its own study of its potential for tourism, angling and commercial fishing, the board had brought together a draft report which it planned to discuss with all the interested parties before submitting a formal proposal to the Secretary of State.

Mull was the other principal area to which the board tried to apply comprehensive techniques early in its life. In its first year of office, it had commissioned the Macaulay Institute for Soil Research to carry out a soil and land use capability survey in the Ross of Mull and had persuaded DAFS and the Forestry Commission to undertake a land survey of the whole island.

Originally the board hoped that the survey would be completed quickly but 1967 came and went without the report coming to hand. It was beginning to learn that it was not to be allowed to carry all before it, and that powerful vested interests on the island and elsewhere, could exercise a brake on its ambitions. Indeed its report[11] for 1968 began to speak of reservations; referring to both Kildonan and Mull it said, 'These comprehensive surveys are pioneering efforts and valuable lessons are being learned. At the same time, it must be stressed that there is no magic formula for transforming poorly endowed areas—and there are many such areas in the Highlands.'

The other main strand in the board's efforts to make the land of the Highlands and islands more productive was provided by its hopes to 'initiate agricultural developments in particular geographical areas or commodity sectors'. By the time it had stated this clearly in its bulletin of October 1968, it had done enough work to justify high hopes of bringing off just such a development in the Uists. In the spring and summer of 1967 it had appointed four young project officers. This was a breed new to the public service. Their remit was to find, research and develop schemes which could attract investment from both the Board and the private sector.

Initially the four were allocated areas of interest haphazardly. Robin Dean, onto whose desk the agricultural portfolio landed, had no previous experience of the industry. This proved an advantage as, without preconceptions, his enthusiasm and hard work led him to produce a project which, for imagination as well as potential future dividends, was to be matched very rarely in the board's experience. Dean's idea was based on work done in the 'fifties by the West of Scotland College of Agriculture on the Inner Hebridean islands of Tiree, Colonsay and Coll in the growing of daffodils, tulips and hyacinths. Hebridean Bulb Growers Ltd had been formed as a cooperative in 1957 and, over the next eight years, it had seen bulb acreage expand to about 20 and the number of growers from 14 to 25. At that point, it failed to convince the board that it was worthy of support and that it was capable of achieving further expansion. It was wound up in 1966.

Out of that apparent failure, Dean was convinced a new, sounder development could come. In his view the keys to success would be concentration of production and highly organised marketing. Six acres were planted in North Uist in the autumn of 1967; the bulbs were lifted in the following summer and were, according to the board, 'of excellent quality'.[12] A further 20 acres were planted that autumn and the board was encouraged in its belief that 'given expert management, large scale but concentrated bulb growing in the Hebrides could be a profitable undertaking'.[13]

Comprehensive development

Comprehensive development was an objective ideally suited to the board. It had been given, unlike later state agencies, a blanket remit which enabled it to influence every aspect of life within the Highlands and islands. Nothing was excluded from its gaze, hardly an activity beyond its financial help. But it was with some reluctance that it embarked on its early work in this field which concerned first, the Strath of Kildonan, and second, the Island of Mull. Both cases were recommended to the board by the Advisory Panel and the Scottish Office.

The board's report[14] on the strath was published in 1970. Explaining its interest, it noted, 'Because of the history of the Clearances, absentee land-ownership and apparent under-use of land resources, the Strath has been frequently cited as a typical example of mis-use of land in the Highlands. Its development along comprehensive land use lines was suggested by the former Advisory Panel on the Highlands and Islands and was recommended by the Scottish Office to the Highlands and Islands Development Board at its inception.

'For these historical reasons, and not because of any particular resources or combination of resources readily suitable for a comprehensive development scheme, the board resolved to take action.' The action was directed towards a programme of research and consultation aimed at producing a set of proposals upon which all the parties involved could work. At the end of it all the board confessed that 'the various comprehensive surveys which have been carried out confirm that the present feasibility of resource development in this area is limited, and much of it is not of a strictly commercial nature'. Undaunted it managed to recommend action in several areas. It recommended that sympathetic consideration should be given to assisting any small-scale manufacturing or processing project which might be suggested for, or within reach of, the village of Helmsdale, particularly if it was relatively flexible in its labour requirements.

On land use it proposed a programme of approximately 15,000 acres of afforestation phased over two ten-year periods and that each of the six estates in the glen should contribute. To increase the output of agriculture it suggested that the improvement of 1500 acres of land should be undertaken.

In fishing it advocated that a new seine net boat should be added to the Helmsdale fleet and that the small-boat fishermen should be encouraged to diversify into crab fishing.

For the tourism business 'modest development on a number of lines' were suggested. These included improved amenity and recreational facilities; a small museum, featuring gold and local history, and facilities for visitors to take part in panning for gold on Suisgill Estate. These, with the exception perhaps of the land use recommendations, were fairly modest proposals. But if the board's approach were to be judged successful then it would have to make progress on what was regarded as the central concern—that of improving land use in the Strath.

On that score there was disappointment. In 1978, seeking more effective powers over rural land use,[15] the board itself commented: 'In the Strath of Kildonan, one of the major recommendations made in the light of a comparison of returns from other land uses as well as employment considerations, was a programme of afforestation, extending at the end of 20 years to 15,000 acres. Since the board's report was discussed with Strath landowners and published, some afforestation has taken place. The paucity of it, however, cannot be disguised and the board sees only a small proportion of the recommended land being afforested either by the Forestry Commission or privately.'

Of Mull, the Advisory Panel in its report of 1964 had said, 'We have given much thought to the problems of Mull, where severe depopulation has taken place and where the standard of agriculture has suffered from a marked trend towards the grouping of farms and from the merging of farms into sporting estates. It has been clear for some time that unless something radical is done, the Island of Mull will have declined to the point at which the revival of community life and a viable economy might no longer be possible.' It was an invitation that the board could not refuse and it responded by setting out to prepare a comprehensive study and development scheme for the island. These[16] were published in 1973, though they had been shaped finally over a year earlier.

The main recommendations were:

LAND USE: the more intensive use of existing enclosed land and the improvement of about 600 acres a year of additional land enabling the livestock output of Mull to rise by an average of three to four per cent a
year during the next decade; continued forestry planting at the then
current rate of 1200 acres a year for at least the next ten years thus
helping to maintain employment for the labour force.

FISHERIES: additional methods of fishing for vessels over 40; the upgrading of
the small boat fleet; development of rainbow trout fish farming;
development of raft cultivation of mussels; depending on the success of the previous two, consideration to be given to the setting up
of a processing plant; the establishment of a fisheries association
representing all aspects of the industry.

TOURISM: new and improved accommodation, ranging from bed and breakfast
to hotels and chalets; adequate restaurant facilities; more and better
organised recreational activities; roll/on, roll/off ferries.

MANUFACTURING: the promotion of crafts and possibly other modest ventures if entrepreneurs could be found and given special guidance.

These were the areas in which the board could act directly. In others,
such as transport and housing, it made recommendations which would be
the responsibility of other agencies.[17] To put as much steam behind its ideas
as possible, however, it made what at the time was a unique proposal to the
Secretary of State.

'Finding an effective means of implementing the recommendations and
proposals,' it told him, 'is all important. The board see their role as helping
to promote individual projects giving financial assistance where
appropriate and acting in concert with others in achieving the desired ends
for the social and economic development of Mull.' It therefore recommended that 'authority be given to appoint a resident official in Mull for a
number of years to assist in the implementation of agreed developments;
and to take the necessary action to establish a Mull Development Committee'. The Scottish Office accepted both recommendations. The official was
appointed in June 1974 and the post was still operative at the end of 1980.
The Mull Development Committee held its first meeting in 1974 and was
disbanded in 1978 to make way for the new community council. The board
hoped that these administrative innovations would give cohesion to its
efforts which would benefit also from a much stronger local input. Having
a presence on Mull ought also to increase the number of cases coming
forward to the board for financial assistance.

In the event these aspirations were realised only partially. Following
the arrival of the Mull Development Officer, Jack Gibson, there was an
increase in the number of applications coming forward for the board's

consideration. Through time, there was a better understanding among islanders of just what the board could and could not do. But the development committee tended to reflect rather than bridge the social divisions within the community.

On the central issue, the concern which had given rise to the apprehension of the Advisory Panel and which had prompted the board into action in the first place, there was dismal progress. In its document on changes in its land use powers the board recorded: 'Despite the survey, its recommendations, the discussions which have surrounded it and all the incentives which the board can offer to development projects, the island still provides many examples of communities and land suffering at the hands of owners whose goals and policies are in conflict with the needs and desires of the community. Concern is increased when one sees that in several cases the land is in poor heart because of recent ownership changes which have allowed new policies condemning the land and the people it supports. In other cases, degeneration of once viable units has taken place gradually but inexorably over decades of misuse.'[18]

Thus by its own standards the board had failed in its comprehensive approach to the two areas which it regarded as an inheritance from the Advisory Panel. It could reasonably hope for more if it itself were to choose an area for examination, one that initially at least might hold out some prospect of success. Understandably the board considered that if it chose an area to which it could apply the techniques of comprehensive development, rather than have to accept for political or other reasons suggestions from outside sources, then it would stand a better chance of success. There would be no prior misconceptions nor would it give rise to unwarranted expectations.

After careful deliberation it decided that Ardnamurchan offered the best opportunities. In 1971 it agreed to go ahead with a survey as a preliminary to comprehensive development proposals.

Carrying the decision into practice beyond the confines of its Inverness headquarters was not so simple as was first, perhaps, expected. The board gave the work no special priority so that its land use staff were unable to allocate other tasks a proper share of their resources. As time went on, the lack of progress with the earlier schemes for Mull and Kildonan also prompted doubts about the sense of the course upon which they had embarked.

The survey of the Ardnamurchan peninsula gained brief mentions in five consecutive annual reports from 1972 but thereafter disappeared. It was never finished, a victim of the board's lack of direction as well as of its experience in failing to make its other comprehensive plans stick.

Though some parts of the survey were to prove useful, the exercise was forgotten quietly. By 1980 comprehensive development were words rarely heard on the lips of board members or their spokesmen.

Projects

In its Occasional Bulletin of October 1968, the board said that it would initiate agricultural projects in particular geographical areas or commodity sectors. 'Where appropriate,' it explained, 'the board may implement such a project itself or seek to achieve that end in cooperation with one or more existing bodies with experience and responsibilities in the relevant field.'

Its first venture in this field was the bulb growing scheme developed by Robin Dean from his work on assessing an application from the cooperative Hebridean Bulb Growers to the board for financial assistance. Bulbs first had been seen as a possible crop in the Hebrides by Dr A R Nisbet, of the West of Scotland College of Agriculture. Under his guidance trials on Tiree, Coll and Colonsay in the early 'fifties had been successful and, in 1956, fourteen crofters and one farmer had agreed to grow trial stock on Tiree and Coll.

Out of that sprang, the following year, Hebridean Bulb Growers Ltd, but its high hopes faltered against the harsh economic and business problems that so often confront an enterprise that is founded on vision and little else.

According to Dean, forecast sales were never achieved and most of the cooperative's grower members failed to make a profit. After 1960, the number of growers fell and, in an attempt to revive its fortunes, the HBG, with a loan of £6000 from the government through the Development Commission, set up a contract scheme. But the writing was on the wall. A reluctant commission was forced to conclude that the project was unlikely to be viable and in 1965 the cooperative voted to wind itself up. But in that year and the following one, results improved to the extent that members agreed to postpone that action and apply to the board for help.

By that time it was clear, to Dean and several others, that the cooperative had failed because it had lacked capital, it had encouraged the dispersal of members rather than their concentration, it had been based on part-time endeavour by its members, it had suffered from the absence of strong, central control and it had lacked experience. Dean travelled the length and breadth of the UK and into Holland conducting his research. He spoke to growers, salesmen, buyers and accountants, technical experts and government officials and crofters and farmers. To the board he recommended[19] that they turn down the request from HBG which, in June 1966,

82 HIGHLAND EXPERIMENT

was looking for about £8000 of grants and around £120,000 of loans. Instead, he submitted, the board should set out to establish a soundly-based, well-managed bulb growing industry in the islands.

Initially the loan capital required would be in excess of £300,000—this at a time when the board was severely restricted in the finance it could offer to one project. But Dean saw his scheme making a major and lasting contribution to the economic and social well-being of the Highlands. The board was not bowled over entirely by Dean's enthusiasm, though members agreed that his work was impressive and demanded further study. In 1967 it appointed Dutch consultants to examine the Vallay Strand in North Uist with a view to assessing its potential, once reclaimed, as a bulb growing area. This was home from home for the Dutch. The Strand is a tidal bay and presented problems similar to those overcome in the construction of fertile polders in Holland. It was not surprising, therefore, when they produced answers which would have been familiar in The Hague. They envisaged damming the Strand to reclaim about 1600 acres, just under half of which would be devoted to bulb growing and a further 400 acres given over to an irrigation storage reservoir.

Meanwhile, the board had set about trials on the machair of North Uist. Daffodils, tulips, crocus and hyacinths brought brilliant colour to that corner of the Hebrides as well as hope of new enterprise and a fresh source of income. In 1967 some six acres were planted around Paible; in 1968, 23; in 1969, 33. 'The results both in quality and quantity,' said the board, 'were excellent.'

In 1969 the board submitted a formal proposal to the Secretary of State, seeking his blessing to a scheme which would reclaim the Vallay Strand, set up a company and establish a production unit. It was an impressive plan, forecasting a rate of return between 6.5 and 9 per cent and claiming a spin-off in a healthier tourism trade. But the board found it could not produce the evidence that the Minister's technical advisers felt they needed. And they could not produce it without first reclaiming part of the Strand. The board's experimental work was being conducted on the machair and the results from that, according to DAFS officials, could not be used as evidence of likely results from reclaimed land. There was no way round that objection. Though work went on until 1972, the board withdrew its proposal in 1971.

According to John Bryden and George Houston,[21] 'insufficient experimental work had been carried out before the project was launched and it seems probable that the only way to carry out such experiments properly to the satisfaction of all would have been to reclaim a part of the Vallay

Strand and lay on irrigation.' To others in the board at the time it seemed that DAFS, not happy about the initiative from the start, had chosen a condition for its blessing which it was impossible to fulfil.

The board ran two other smaller experimental projects during the 'seventies. In 1970, following discussions with the North of Scotland College of Agriculture and others, it decided to set up a pilot project to assess the possibilities for growing blueberries. The site chosen was on the Black Isle where five acres of highbush blueberries, most of them bought from the US, were planted.

Very early in its development it ran into management problems, with sharp differences of opinion arising between the board's consultant and the Scottish Horticultural Research Institute which, in August 1972, had undertaken an assessment of the project for the board. From the following May, day to day management was taken over by the North of Scotland College. By that time the board had reported, that despite a weed problem, there were 'encouraging signs that the bushes had become well established and were beginning to grow satisfactorily'.[22] When the College took over all the bushes were lifted and the whole five acres deep-ploughed, harrowed and rolled. The older bushes were replanted and the younger ones moved to a nursery site at the College's grounds in Inverness. This work overcame the weeds but the project then faced a difficulty in getting enough new bushes to plant in its remaining acreage, a shortage it resolved by obtaining supplies from the SHRI at Invergowrie.

In 1975 the first small crop was taken and by the following year enough ground had been planted to permit both fruiting trials and propagation of supplies. Though the plantation suffered from accidental spray damage, the first worthwhile crop—more than 150 lb—was picked in the autumn of 1977. Processors were reported to be pleased with the size, cleanliness, general appearance and quality of the fruit. Unfortunately, this success was shortlived with severe late frosts cutting back on the production of berries. Early in 1979 the board decided to kill the scheme on the grounds that the uncertainty of production 'was unlikely to attract commercial exploitation by fruit growers in the area'.[23] It was taken over by the owner of the land in 1980 who enjoyed a good crop which he was able to sell locally.

The board met with more success in its experimental work in shrub growing. In 1970, with technical advice being supplied by the West of Scotland College of Agriculture, it set up a pilot scheme at Ormsary on ground leased from Sir William Lithgow, one of whose companies was to act as the marketing outlet for the enterprise.

By 1975 progress had been so marked that a new company, Highland

Heathers Ltd, had been established to develop production at a site at Achahoish, Knapdale. The project at Ormsary meanwhile was run down and eventually closed in March 1977, 'Over its seven year life,' the board claimed, 'sales from the unit broadly carried the costs, and the project was influential in the establishment of at least two new sizeable commercial shrub production schemes in Argyll.'[24]

Deer farming

On 23 February 1977, the board announced that, for £275,000, it had bought Rahoy, an estate of 3800 acres in Morvern in the West Highlands in order to test the feasibility of farming red deer commercially.

Eight years previously, along with the Rowett Research Institute of Aberdeen, it had organised a conference[25] to examine the question. Out of that had come the experimental farm at Glensaugh, Kincardineshire, which was managed jointly by the Institute and the Hill Farming Research Organisation. The work at Glensaugh had shown that farming deer seemed to be a practical proposition but required to be tested in conditions which resembled more closely those which would be experienced by a commercial operator.

Rahoy was to provide these conditions.

The board set out three main objectives for its project:

1   to develop and test commercially applicable deer farming systems that would be of practical relevance for development in the Highlands and Islands;

2   to investigate the performance of farmed deer under West Highland conditions, taking as a base the practices evolved at Glensaugh;

3   to act as a demonstration unit for intending deer farmers and a source of breeding stock for commercial farms.

Clearly Rahoy would produce its dividends in the long term. Simply obtaining the basic stock of 400 hinds, it was reckoned, would take up to three to four years.

To oversee the work, the board set up its own management team to which the farm manager was to be responsible. Supporting that group was an additional committee, consisting of representatives of the HFRO, RRI, the North of Scotland College of Agriculture, DAFS and the Red Deer Commission, which was to advise the board on policy, on the running of the project and on the results obtained from it.

During 1978 the stock of the farm grew to 200 while is area was extended by fencing to just under 350 hectares. A further hill paddock was fenced during the summer of 1979, and in the following year the total area was doubled. On it, stocking was completed with 404 hinds of all ages and 112 stags. The board reported that the project was 'now entering the phase in which the large-scale farming systems originally envisaged will be evaluated'.[26] Problems with growth and calving forced changes in the original system; to avoid loss of weight during the winter, breeding hinds were given more winter feed while only calves to be used to replace breeding stock were wintered on the farm. The board also found that it had underestimated the costs of running the enterprise; this was particularly so with salaries and wages, maintenance and parts of the fencing programme. Despite that experience it hoped, at the beginning of 1982, that costs over the following two years would be reduced substantially so that, after allowing for inflation, the total expenditure of £260,000 initially forecast for the seven years of the scheme would not be over-run.

Agriculture

The board was always clear that it ought to encourage more intensive and more efficient farming methods. In 1969 DAFS approved a scheme whereby it could use its grants and loans to achieve that end. Loans were to be made available for the erection or adaptation of buildings, the purchase of plant and equipment and the provision of working capital for an agreed programme of development. Capital repayments could be deferred while interest free periods were also an option if the board considered them justified. The criteria which the board was to take into account included the technical feasibility of the project as well as its expected rate of return. It would also take into consideration, as it did with its schemes of assistance to other sectors, the financial resources and the managerial ability of the applicant. Grants were to be rare, unless to supplement a loan or to finance a project which, though it could be of special development value, was unable to get assistance from another source.

In 1977,[27] the board claimed, 'The results which grants and loans have so far produced are on the whole encouraging. Ninety per cent of the total assistance has been by loans and the bad debt stands at 2.2 per cent, not a high percentage.' Overall, at that time the board had written off over £708,000 or 3.9 per cent of all loans advanced.

On the basis of keeping records of the performance of those farmers in receipt of its help—estimated at one in ten of all full time farmers in the Highlands—the board reckoned that they compared favourably in terms of output and employment with those who though running comparable units, had not taken advantage of the board's assistance. Of significance, too, was the fact that its help had been 'of particular value to younger-than-average farmers with heavier-than-average financial commitments. The selective nature of the assistance has helped to reveal a gap in the capital market for agriculture where regional development considerations are relevant.'

Over the years the board's approach to farming had become a great deal more sophisticated. By 1977 it was able to translate it into quite specific agricultural targets. It believed it was 'technically possible to achieve an increase in the production of mutton and lamb from the region of around 2 per cent per annum; by the end of ten years this would mean an addition to total farm output of roughly £3 million per annum at 1976 prices'. For cattle its target was of the same order. If realised it would mean, over a period of ten years, an addition of total output of around £4 million per annum at 1975 prices.

Growth in these sectors, the board considered, would not prevent expansion of seed potato production, dairying, pigs, barley and specialised fruit and vegetables. To achieve these aims the board saw it as necessary to continue its scheme of financial assistance for individual projects, to develop special schemes to provide help to crofters and farmers to improve the quality of lambs and calves sold and to continue monitoring the impact of its assistance coupled with greater technical after care from its own resources.

A later unpublished study, completed in 1980, came to broadly the same conclusions. It told the board, 'The evidence available suggests that board assistance to agriculture in the mid 1970s raised the economic efficiency of selected farm businesses in the Highlands to a new, higher level, thus generating private and social benefits hopefully in excess of its real cost.'

Ownership

In its report in 1964 the Advisory Panel had been blunt about land use. 'Clearly,' it said, 'there is a good deal of under-used, and in some cases grossly mis-used, land in the Highlands. Much of this land could be better used. Highlands and national interest requires that it should be.'[28]

To many that was a reason why its founders gave the board the power to purchase land compulsorily if necessary. In the March 1965 debate in the House of Commons, the Secretary of State, Willie Ross, made the same point. One of the first powers that had to be given to the board, he said was related to the proper use of land itself. 'Anyone who denies that power,' he added, 'is suggesting that the board should not function effectively at all.'[29]

Living up to that expectation proved to be beyond the board. Not that it did not become the owner of substantial tracts of the Highlands and Islands. Rarely did it have difficulty in securing land on which to build factories; part of its package to counter the effects of the failure of the Duncan Logan enterprise in 1971, for example, was taking the company's ground at Muir of Ord into its ownership and turning it into an industrial estate. Nor did it encounter great resistance when it bought from the Forestry Commission the upper slopes of Cairngorm in 1970 the better to develop the area's tourism attractions. And it was fortunate to find a willing seller in the case of Rahoy Estate which it took into the public domain to use as an experimental deer farm. But it was not able to purchase an estate on which it could demonstrate the benefits of progressive land use. Yet, if anything, the need for such a demonstration grew more essential with the passing years. Part of the difficulty was that landowners were able frequently to act as if the twentieth century had not dawned. Lord Strathcona and Mount Royal, proprietor of Colonsay in the Inner Hebrides—and later a junior Minister in the Government of Mrs Margaret Thatcher—gave the board an early example of that.

Late in 1966 Strathcona and his wife visited the board's headquarters at their own request. They explained to their audience that they had been forced to increase rents as income from tenants had fallen by around 50 per cent. Strathcona's family had owned Colonsay for many years and had run it in a patriarchal fashion, but now the pressure of events left the choice either of selling or of altering the island's economy fundamentally. Discussion revolved around possible solutions, with the board under the impression that it had some time in hand. Its representatives agreed at that meeting on 7 November to send an official party, including one board member, to Colonsay in the New Year.

But at the beginning of December the proprietor of the Colonsay Hotel, Barry Davidson, wrote to the board to inform it that the islanders had formed a Ways and Means Committee in an effort 'to try and bring some ray of light that might save the community from disaster'. Their action had been provoked by the landlord who had 'declared all estate workers redundant from the first of January and from that date all estate services and offices were to cease operating'.

Mr Davidson went on to ask the board's help 'to try and bring some hope for a worried population, none of whom can see any hope of a secure living for their children or dependent relatives'. Until that cry for help arrived the board had had no hint that the Strathconas were contemplating such an abrupt step. Throughout all their exchanges with board representatives, the landowners had kept that counsel to themselves.

Another difficulty was that the board could not be sure that it would always come face to face with a willing seller. Though that happened at Rahoy, it was very far from happening in the case of Eigg. This small island of 8000 acres in the Inner Hebrides had fallen into the hands of the Anglyn Trust in 1971. The Trust, under the direction of Bernard Farnham-Smith, paid around £90,000 and claimed to have plans to run on the island an adventure school for handicapped boys. These hopes never matured. In an atmosphere of growing recrimination, Farnham-Smith decided to sell. The board put in an offer only to have it turned down because the Trust did not want the island to go into public ownership.

Instead it was sold to Keith Schellenberg, who successfully ran estates in Aberdeenshire. He paid £270,000 in December 1974 and promptly suggested to the board that, since their interest had raised the price, they should offer him a grant to bridge the difference.

But even where the owner had no political prejudices about the likely buyers of his land, the board also could find itself prevented from acting because of political pressure from the Government.

On Mull, Killiechronan ran to about 9500 acres and, in its hey day, contained five tenant farms. By 1975 its future was uncertain. It was up for sale and, according to the Glasgow Herald, the residents of Mull were 'up in arms' about the prospect of changes that would deprive the island of the estate's jobs.[30]

Because of its earlier work and research on Mull, the board was aware of the estate's potential. In seeking the Secretary of State's permission to make an offer it prepared extensive papers for the Scottish Office setting out its plans should its bid be successful. After lengthy discussion, re-examination and consultation the Scottish Office eventually agreed to the board's proposal. The board was confident that it was on the verge of making a fundamental breakthrough. It understood that its offer of around £275,000 would be acceptable to the estate; it had the money in its budget though that would require some internal re-adjustment to release the funds; and its political master once more was Willie Ross who, in setting up the board ten years before, had shown that he was aware of the need for it to tackle the deep-rooted problem of land use.

But the board had not reckoned with the Treasury. Harold Wilson's third administration was going through one of those exercises which were to become a familiar feature of the 'seventies—a cut in public spending. Although the case for the HIDB's purchase of Killiechronan was put by Bruce Millan, Ross's second in command at the Scottish Office, the Treasury was not to be moved. Spending such an amount on such a scheme

would be an embarrassment, it seemed, to the Government. The answer
was no. The Secretary of State was not prepared to demonstrate his
independence. He it was who took the burden, the board observing drily,
'. . . In this instance the approval of the Secretary of State was not granted
because of the difficult public expenditure situation.' It went on ruefully,
'We have maintained close contact with the new owner of Killiechronan in
an attempt to influence the policy for the estate as best we can within our
existing powers.'[31]

The board and the people of Mull had much to rue.

The new owner was David Holman, an insurance broker, whose aim was
to run Killiechronan as a sporting estate. Within a year he had cut the
number of jobs available from 22 to 2 and had reduced the stock the estate
carried.

But Raasay was the island that was to epitomise the issue of obstructive
ownership. Russell Johnstons' intervention in 1966, when he advised Bob
Grieve, the HIDB's chairman, to use the board's power of compulsory
purchase to buy out Green, was too early for the board. It was not until
1967 that its representatives visited the island and it was not until 1979 that
the Gordian knot of Green's ownership was cut. The intervening years
were spent in dealing with a recalcitrant landlord who seemed determined
to obstruct development. Green objected to plans for a ferry terminal,
turned down offers to buy his properties and, at times, seemed to cover the
whole island with his dead hand. Yet he owned less than 200 acres of
Raasay. It was 1968 before the board sought and obtained permission from
the Secretary of State to try to wrest them from his grasp.

In 1969 the board set up a working party, including representatives of
the island community, to examine development possibilities. The result of
its deliberations was a fairly modest programme of investment which
hinged on the provision of an improved ferry service. In October of that
year Prophet Smith, the board member who had chaired the working
group, revealed the chief ingredients of the programme at a press conference. The board's intention was to spend £110,000 in two years on projects
based on Raasay's tourism and fishing potential. All but £30,000 was to be
directed towards tourist accommodation while the balance was to be spent
developing the island's clam and prawn resources.[32]

But the improvement in transport services was nowhere in sight. Still on
the drawing board was a plan agreed by Inverness County Council, DAFS,
MacBraynes and the HIDB for a ferry capable of carrying four vehicles and
25 passengers. Two years later this proposal had been developed to include
provision of landing stages, offices, moorings and a breakwater at a cost of

over £100,000. In what was now the familiar Raasay manner, this scheme was debated and disputed, mainly because of its cost and how it would be shared between central government and local agencies. In the autumn of 1971—more than three years after the initial plan gained the assent of all the interested parties—it was agreed to pursue a modified version in the hope of approaching the target of the major scheme gradually over a number of years.

But the first step could not be contemplated, thanks to Dr Green who was not prepared to release the land needed for the ferry terminal. This was to prove a stumbling block for the next four years. The board was clear that it would be foolish to proceed with their November 1969 proposals in the absence of an improved ferry service. This was confirmed in the spring of 1972 by Sir Andrew Gilchrist, its chairman, when he assured the islanders that immediately the first brick of the new ferry terminal was laid on Raasay, the board would go ahead with its project. Immediately after giving that commitment, Gilchrist met Green in Edinburgh. Though the press saw the board party—and representatives of Inverness County Council—they did not catch sight of the elusive man they by now called Dr No. He had arrived at the solicitor's office early and by a back door.

The outcome of these exchanges seemed favourable. Raasay's best known landlord said that not only was he prepared to negotiate the sale of the land required by the county for the ferry terminal, but he was also ready to go to arbitration on a price for the sale to the board of all his property on the island.[33]

Inverness County Council pressed on, encouraged by Lord Burton[34] who was the chairman of its Roads Committee and who, some suggested, was anxious to proceed because he thought that Green was giving landowners a bad name. What the council needed amounted to 955 square yards of ground and what they offered, after advice from the district valuer, was £10. It met with silence from Bexhill-on-Sea. Councillors agreed to an ultimatum but that brought no response by the given date. In June 1972, the council agreed to go for a compulsory purchase order. Inevitably Dr Green objected. The Secretary of State, Gordon Campbell, set the public enquiry for Portree in March 1973. Eight months later, on the basis of the reporter's findings, he confirmed the order. The council was free to go ahead. Or so it thought.

Dr Green appealed against the Minister's decision to the Court of Session. This was not heard until 26 June 1975 when Dr Green and his wife objected on archaeological, maritime and historical grounds. When the court re-assembled to continue the hearing on 2 July it was informed that the claimants were abandoning their case.

Figure 10. Sheep shearing near Leverburgh

But there was to be yet another twist. Highland Region, which had incorporated Inverness County Council on reorganisation, established that, because of the legal delays, the cost of the project had risen beyond its means. A month after Dr Green had abandoned his objection, the region abandoned the project, deciding instead to build a landing hard and a wave screen at the existing pier.[35]

Throughout this period the HIDB was not sitting on its hands. After all, Dr Green had accepted the idea of going to arbitration. But the District Valuer's price, which the board could not exceed, was not good enough. Dr Green described the offer as 'ridiculous'. By this time the board was well aware of how difficult Dr Green could be in negotiation. The pattern became repetitive. Just when a breakthrough seemed on hand, new conditions would emerge that put everything back in the melting pot.

To confound matters further, he submitted plans for a £½ million tourist development, involving two hotels, staff accommodation, a garage and filling station—evidence that he believed his thesis that facilities on the island should come first, better transport second. These were refused planning permission in December 1973.

The previous month the board had been advised by George Younger, a junior Minister at the Scottish Office, to have one more try at negotiating a solution. Speaking in an adjournment debate in the House of Commons in November,[36] he had said that if the attempt failed then the board had compulsory powers to hand.

The HIDB carried on, occasionally, when asked by the press, confirming that they were still negotiating. But soon it set its sights on buying Borrodale House, dropping its original notion of buying all of Green's properties. It also devised and published a plan to build a small hotel of 22 rooms on a site which lay about 500 yards to the north of Raasay House and which was owned by the Secretary of State. Never at a loss, it seemed, Green had a shed erected on the spot. That was in August 1977. By the end of the year the logjam had been broken. The board purchased Borrodale from Green for £16,000 and immediately sent a team to Raasay to explain its plans to the community. It took another year to pull together a scheme for the property's conversion into a 15-room hotel able to cope with 33 guests and to have it approved by the Scottish Office.

Several weeks later, on 8 April 1979, the board announced that it had bought all of Dr Green's remaining properties on the island in a deal that cost £135,000. Green said he was sad to break his connection with the island. The board was delighted. But it hesitated. Should it proceed with Borrodale, the conversion of which had been approved by the Secretary of

State in February, or were there better possibilities still in Raasay House? The islanders had to wait a little longer before they heard that the Borrodale project was to proceed. It opened under the direction of a local woman and her daughter in July 1981—a year behind the original schedule while Raasay House was leased to a charitable trust which was to run it as an adventure school.

In confronting what all its supporters, including its political founders, saw as the key problem of Highland development the board had been flawed fatally from the start. The Secretary of State, Willie Ross, had seen that it was given compulsory purchase powers but the act, which he pushed through Parliament in a period when the administration of which he was a member had a majority of only three in the Commons, made it clear that it could use that power only in terms of the Acquisition of Land (Authorisation Procedure) (Scotland) Act 1947.[37]

This meant, essentially, that the board would enjoy the same powers as those of a local authority. But where a council found these provisions sufficient to allow it to acquire ground for a particular building or for a road improvement the board was to find them of no help at all in trying to reach its objectives. The board wanted to obtain land on which it could demonstrate a comprehensive approach to better land use. To do that it required estates measured in thousands of acres, not small pockets of ground. When eventually it sought legal advice on the point it was told fairly bluntly that it would not win its case. It did not have the power to do so.

Why then did it not attempt to demonstrate that its powers were inadequate so that it then could ask for more?

During Bob Grieve's chairmanship, the question did not present itself in that way. For most of that period, ending in 1970, the question of owner-ship had focused on Dr Green and his minute acreage on Raasay. The board had been authorised to negotiate with him and the negotiations were to carry on beyond Grieve's period of office. By then, a new Government was in Westminster under Edward Heath who had appointed Gordon Campbell as his Secretary of State. Coincidentally there was also a new chairman of the HIDB, Sir Andrew Gilchrist, who had spent his career in the diplomatic service. Initially he was not enthusiastic about the board's powers of compulsory purchase. He believed that land needed for the board's economic purposes 'could almost invariably be acquired in a different way . . . with much less fuss and wear and tear'.[38]

In so far as the board was believed to have been given these powers so that it could tackle the wider question of landownership and land use, he regarded it as 'an unfortunate and impracticable commitment'. '. . . The land to be acquired,' he argued, 'had to be paid for at its full value, so that the percentage of Highland land which the board, with its existing annual income, could acquire would be completely negligible; thus, in the doubtful hope of creating or altering a few jobs in the Highlands, the board would find itself at the storm centre of not merely a legal but a political struggle which ought to have been fought out in Parliament and not left to a few non-political appointees like myself.'

There was the additional difficulty that, for the first four years of his term, a Conservative Government was in power. An application to a Tory Secretary of State, he felt, would not be likely to meet with success. Despite these reservations, Sir Andrew Gilchrist, in common with his colleagues, the board's political founders and outside observers, thought that the powers existed. And Raasay persuaded him to make use of them. 'I was well aware of the legal resistance which might be made,' he recalls, 'but I relied on the conspicuous contrast between our own development plans and the stagnation and dereliction under the existing ownership; surely we could defeat a bad landlord and take over his land by exhibiting our legal powers and by proving we would be a better landlord.

'It gradually emerged, after legal consultation, that the position had been misunderstood and that, for reasons now generally accepted, for the purpose of taking over a generalised or multifarious activity like an estate, the alleged powers were for all practical purposes, worthless.'

He entertained no hope for change. No political party he thought would ever provide the board with powers appropriate to the task. To try to persuade politicians to enact special legislation which would discriminate between Highland landlords and all other landlords in the UK and entrust the administration of such discrimination to the HIDB would be a waste of time and energy. The board would have to reach its objectives through the powers of inducement and demonstration, not the power of compulsory purchase.

When Kenneth Alexander took over as chairman in 1976 which appointment, once more, had been made by a Labour Government, he was not aware of the strength of the legal advice the board had received. Within a year of moving from his post as Professor of Economics at Strathclyde University to Inverness he established that in the view of the Scottish Office, 'practical proof of the inadequacy of the board's compulsory purchase powers was not an essential preliminary to the consideration of legislation amending the board's powers'.[39] On that understanding he moved, along with John Bryden,[40] Head of the board's Land Development Division, to produce a set of proposals for submission to the Secretary of State.

The subject of consultation with the Scottish Landowners' Federation and the National Farmers' Union, this was published in 1978 after the Secretary of State, Bruce Millan, had asked that further discussion of the scheme should take place. As Alexander and his colleagues saw it, the proposal would make effective the powers Parliament had given in the 1965 act; the augmented powers it suggested were designed exclusively to deal with 'extreme cases of underuse or misuse of land', while the processes envisaged would provide for a consensus of opinion from both professional and local sources.

Under the board's proposals an area of land first would have to be designated as one in which the use of the powers the board was seeking would lead to changes in land use consistent with the board's strategy. A proposal to designate could come from the board itself, but also from local councils, or branches of the NFU or SLF, or any group resident in the area representing at least 10 per cent of the electoral roll.

Once the board had accepted the case for designation, a local advisory committee and a technical panel would be set up. The first would consist of nominees of the local authorities, SLF, NFU, Scottish TUC and the board; the second would have representatives from the colleges of agriculture, DAFS, Hill Farming Research Organisation, Royal Institute of Chartered Surveyors, the Institute of Foresters of Great Britain and where warranted, the Red Deer Commission and the Crofters Commission. In consultation with both committees the board would draw up a draft outline development plan for the area. The draft would be sent to all owners and occupiers of land in the area and discussions would be opened with all of those affected by the plan. The local Advisory Committee would hear objections from any owner or occupier who contested the proposals. Along with the technical panel, it would offer comments to the board as well as records of any hearings. On that basis, the board would amend the plan and publish it locally. With the LAC it would hold a public meeting, following which it would submit to the Secretary of State the plan and a record of any hearings related to unresolved issues.

If the Minister approved the development plan the area would be designated by order of the Secretary of State and the board would be empowered to use within it not only its existing powers but also the following:

1   the power of nominated leasing by which land could be leased out if the board scheduled it;

2   the power of controlling the sale of land by which transactions would have to be

reported to the board so that it could approve, in the light of the proposals in the plan, the prospective buyer's plans for the land;

3   the power of compulsory purchase which would be an instrument of last resort, used only when all other means had failed.

After carrying out the second round of consultation demanded by Bruce Millan, the board submitted its proposals, with some slight changes, to him in December 1978. So far, the Minister had not shown any anxiety to come quickly to the board's assistance. He had received the first document in February but did not discuss it with the board until June. And at that point he had requested another round of consultations, so ensuring the loss of another six months. Whether he was stalling or whether the delay was the fault of his advisers is difficult to judge.

Certainly the James Callaghan Government, of which he was a member, was shipping a great deal of water. The pact[41] with the Liberals under David Steel, which had kept it afloat from the spring of 1977, had ended and the Government increasingly had to rely on deals with all the minority parties. Among the most cooperative of these was the Scottish National Party which was prepared to stay in line until the referendum[42] on the Scottish Assembly had taken place. It was that issue which more than any other dominated thinking among politicians and civil servants in New St Andrew's House towards the end of 1978. Yet presumably the Scottish Nationalist as well as the Liberal MPs would have supported any attempt by Callaghan's Scottish team to strengthen the HIDB. The leader of the SNP in Parliament was Donald Stewart, who represented the Western Isles, while Russell Johnston, MP for Inverness-shire, who had advocated to the board the use of their existing powers against Dr Green on Raasay, was still a senior member of the Liberal contingent.

When the board's plans arrived on Bruce Millan's desk for a second time they got no further than the pending tray. They were still there when George Younger moved in as a member of the new Conservative administration in May 1979.

Younger had been a junior Minister at the Scottish Office in Heath's Government. He it was who, in the course of the adjournment debate on the Raasay question in November 1973, had suggested that since the Secretary of State had approved the compulsory purchase order raised by Inverness County Council against Dr Green and therefore had made sure the ferry terminal would be built, the board should attempt once more to negotiate with the landowner. If that proved fruitless then, he pointed out, the compulsory power procedure was open to the board.

Now, in 1979, a member of a Government which was uncompromising in its hostility to public enterprise, he was in no hurry to give an opinion on the board's new proposals. But eventually he did. On 7 May 1980,[43] almost a year to the day since he had taken office, he was asked in the House of Commons by Robert Maclennan, then Labour MP for Caithness but soon to become the first Scottish member to join the Social Democratic Party, if he was to seek to increase the powers of the board over the use of land. Younger replied, 'No, sir. The HIDB has similar powers to those of other public agencies and local authorities and I am not persuaded that there is need to extend them.'

Maclennan persisted. 'Does that mean that the Secretary of State rejects the legal advice given to the Scottish Office, which was accepted by his predecessor . . . ? Does the Secretary of State agree that it would be wholly unreasonable to ask the HIDB to put to use powers that it has, only to demonstrate their complexity? Does the Secretary of State accept or reject that legal advice or has he received fresh legal advice?'

'No, sir,' Younger replied. 'The legal advice is there and I have no reason to quarrel with it. The honourable gentleman asks whether I wish to give new powers to the HIDB. I was making it clear that, if existing powers have not been used, I see no reason to give further powers to the board.'

In response to Donald Stewart, who thought it was incredible that the Minister should be satisfied with the situation, Younger attempted to clarify his attitude. 'The Highlands and Islands Development Board has wide powers,' he said. 'If the board has not so far used those powers it would be strange if parliament were asked to give it yet more powers without due cause shown.'

He agreed with John Mackay, Argyll's Conservative MP, who put the matter very clearly when he asked Younger if he would restate that he, and the HIDB, had powers to deal with those matters raised by the board in their document seeking augmented powers. 'The board has never attempted to use those powers and until it does attempt to use them it should not seek additional powers.'

Thus, in the course of a brief exchange across the floor of the House of Commons, the board had been returned to square one. After fifteen years it had made no progress on the issue which its friends and foes alike saw as central to its work.

But no outcry came from the board's headquarters in Inverness. The *West Highland Free Press* called upon Sir Kenneth Alexander to challenge the decision publicly before he demitted office. 'If even the most obnoxious powers of landlords are to be jealously protected by their Tory friends,' it said, 'then this should be made clear to the people of the Highlands and Islands. On this issue above all, Sir Kenneth should go out fighting.'[44] The chairman was not to be drawn.

He had started out on his term declaring that he would be surprised if no progress were made with the issue during his period as chairman. He had spent much of his time throughout the following five years devising the set of proposals which the Secretary of State turned down. He had as much reason as anyone to complain, not only about the politicians but also about the senior officials in the Scottish Office who not only had advised him that a demonstration of the weakness of the board's existing powers would not be needed in order to have them changed but also had stalled for months prior to the election.

None of his frustration spilled over in public. He recognised[45] later that perhaps that made him appear 'more chicken' than he really was, but he claimed that he made his position clear in the course of a meeting with the Highland Region. The region's minute[46] of that discussion reads,

> Sir Kenneth said that the board's proposals for changes in their act to allow more effective powers over rural land use had been submitted to the Government in 1978, following extensive consultation with all the main bodies concerned. In 1979 Lord Mansfield, the Minister of State at the Scottish Office, had asked the board to provide evidence of well documented examples of areas where the board would wish to see such powers exercised. This information was provided to the Government some months later. There had been no further discussion at that stage and the board had been surprised when, in March 1980 the Secretary of State, in replying to a parliamentary question, had said that the board would not be given additional powers. He had also said then that, as the board's existing powers had not been used there was no reason to augment the powers already held.
>
> The board had found this answer particularly surprising when they knew that the Government's own advice was that the board's existing powers were inadequate to deal with the types of land use problems which the board had highlighted. It therefore seemed strange for the board to be given advice to try to use these powers.
>
> The board had written to this effect to the Scottish Office. They had replied that, although the Government did not intend to introduce measures to give effect to the board's proposals (as they stood) the continuing exchange on the under-use of land, its extent and causes, had not been closed.

Gilchrist had proved right. It had been a waste of time to pursue the question. The board chose not to make an issue of it and accepted that it could make progress only by example and by inducement. Any other course would be expensive of time, finance and staff.

It was not a battle it had lost, but the war. The injustices inflicted by some landowners on the communities depending on them—and which had been identified by the board itself—would be allowed to continue.

Notes

1   An account of the trial can be found in *The Trial of Patrick Sellar* by Ian Grimble
2   John Kenneth Galbraith, *The Age of Uncertainty*, p 27. BBC/Andre Deutsch, 1927
3   The Report of the Commissioners of Inquiry into the Condition of Crofters and Cottars in the Highlands and Islands of Scotland was published in 1884
4   The Congested Districts Board was set up in 1897 to develop farming and fishing as well as roads and harbours. It ceased its work in 1911, some of its functions being transferred to the Board of Agriculture
5   'Some 35 families or companies with holdings over 36,000 acres therefore account for about one third of all privately owned land in the Highlands and Islands. . . .', *Agrarian Change in the Scottish Highlands*, Bryden and Houston, p 68. According to this source, private landowners control 44 per cent of the total area of agricultural and forestry land. *Glasgow Social and Economic Research Studies 4*, Martin Robertson, 1976. John Bryden and George Houston were at that time Head of the HIDB's Land Development Division and Professor of Agricultural Economics, University of Glasgow, respectively. In addition, Houston was the HIDB's consultant on agricultural matters.
6   Set up in 1946 by the Scottish Secretary, Joseph Westwood, to advise him on plans by Government departments, local authorities and other public agencies for promoting the best economic use of the resources of the Highlands and islands, the panel was an influential voice until it was wound up on the establishment of the board and its consultative council.
7   The board's first annual report covered the period 1 November 1965 to 31 December 1966
8   The Hydro Electric Development Act 1943 formed the NSHEB before the nationalisation of Britain's electricity supply industry in 1948. The board was given the additional duty of collaborating in measures for 'the economic development and social improvement of the area'
9   'A further question by (Russell) Johnston in the House of Commons elicited the fact that Dr Green had only made full payment for the farm which he had bought in 1962 as late as October 1967.' Martin Macdonald, *Glasgow Herald* 14 March 1972
10 Occasional Bulletin no 2, October 1968
11 HIDB, Third Report, 1968, p 59
12 Ibid, p 60
13 Ibid, p 60
14 *Strath of Kildonan, Proposals for Development*, Special Report 5, April 1970
15 Proposals for changes in the Highlands and Islands Development (Scotland) Act 1965 to allow more effective powers over rural land use; a consultative document produced by the HIDB in 1978 'as a basis for formal consultation with organisations and individuals who have an interest in land use in the Highlands and islands'

16   Island of Mull, Survey and Proposals for Development, Special Report 10
     August 1973
17   The report's discussion of transport (pp 67–78) are the best illustration of
     this: it produced 16 recommendations, ranging from urging a roll-on/roll-off
     ferry to suggesting the development of the network of air services. Such
     ideas were for others to pursue.
18   Ibid, p 18
19   *Bulbs from the Western Isles*, a Feasibility Study, Robin Dean
20   HIDB, Fourth Report, 1969, p 4
21   Bryden and Houston, ibid, p 21
22   HIDB, Seventh Report, 1972, p 56
23   HIDB, Fourteenth Report, 1979, p 73
24   HIDB, Twelfth Report, 1977, p 80
25   The proceedings of the conference were published in The Husbanding of
     Red Deer, edited by M M Bannerman and K L Blaxter, HIDB/Rowett
     Research Institute
26   HIDB, Fifteenth Report, 1980, p 80
27   Occasional Bulletin no 7, June 1977
28   *Land use*: a report by the Advisory Panel on the Highlands and Islands, 1964.
29   *Hansard*, Session 1964–5, vol 708, col 1082
30   *Glasgow Herald* 22 August 1975
31   HIDB, Tenth Report, 1975, p 72
32   *The Scotsman* 1 November 1969
33   *The Scotsman* 30 March 1972
34   Lord Burton, Dochfour, owner of some of the most extensive tracts of the
     Highlands and islands, was a prominent member of the old county council
35   *The Scotsman* 22 August 1975; the following day the newspaper reported
     that Dr Green was critical of the council's decision
36   *Hansard*, Session 1973–4, vol 865, col 772
37   Section 4, Clause 2 of the Highlands and Islands Development (Scotland) Act
     1965 reads: The Acquisition of Land (Authorisation Procedure) (Scotland) Act
     1947 shall apply in relation to the compulsory purchase of land by the Board
     as if this Act had been in force immediately before the commencement of
     that Act and as if the Board were a local authority within the meaning of
     that Act
38   This, and the following remarks from Sir Andrew, are taken from a note of
     his views kindly supplied by him to the author
39   Preface, Proposals for changes in the Highlands and Islands Development
     (Scotland) Act 1965
40   John Bryden joined the board as Head of its Land Development Division in
     1972. Following the failure of the board's campaign to improve its powers
     over land use, he resigned in November 1979
41   The Labour-Liberal agreement was announced on 23 March 1977 by James
     Callaghan and David Steel, originally to last until the end of the 1976–7

session. It provided the Labour Government, which had been in a minority
in the House of Commons since April, 1976 with the support it needed to
stay in power, with both parties agreeing to work together 'in the pursuit of
economic recovery'. It was renewed once but lapsed at the end of the
1977–8 session, the Liberals claiming that it had achieved its central purpose
and that they could see no common long term basis for continuing with it

42   The referendum took place on 1 March 1979; those in favour of the
     Government's Scottish devolution proposals gained a small majority which
     was not of sufficient size to overcome the 40 per cent requirement imposed
     by the Scotland Act which, as a result, fell

43   *Hansard*, Session 1978–80, vol 984, cols 263, 264

44   *West Highland Free Press* 25 January 1980

45   Interview with the author, 30 April 1981

46   Highland Regional Council, 3 March 1981, p 1715. These minutes were noted
     at the council's meeting on 22 January 1981 and recorded as an appendix to
     the minutes of that meeting.

CONCLUSION

This board has not got one tooth, but the Secretary of State has got a most ferocious set of snappers

There have been very few attempts to measure the effectiveness of the Highland Board, despite the fact that it is seen to occupy an important place within the Scottish community and to be an institution of some weight. One of the earliest took the form of an essay by Ian Carter, a lecturer in the Department of Sociology at Aberdeen University, in the spring of 1973. Entitled 'Six Years On', it claimed to be an 'evaluative study' of the HIDB.

The central question to which the writer addressed himself was, did the board implement the growth centre policy which it then espoused in theory? Confessing that it was difficult to come to clear views because of the lack of specificity of the statistics produced by the board, he nevertheless managed to conclude that it did not practice what it preached.

> The remarkably large amount of aid which Shetland has received from the board, [he wrote] through careful planning and a great deal of initiative on the part of Shetlanders suggests that we should not view the board as it would like to be viewed, as a thrusting, dynamic combination of research agency and action agency on the TVA model, but rather as a fairly passive milch cow. Perhaps the most dangerous thing which could happen for peripheral areas of the Highlands is that the Highland Board's actions with regard to growth centre policy should match its pretensions.[1]

To the board this sour judgment was a classic example of what happened when an academic ventured out of his ivory tower to be blinded by the light of the real world. The essay seemed to imply that a growth centre policy was valid only if it denied investment totally to those areas not designated as being capable of supporting major development—an implication which obviously could have no political reality. It also ignored completely several existing examples where research and action had been undertaken. There were many criticisms which could have been levelled fairly at the board at that time. Lack of dynamism certainly was not one.

A second assessment appeared in 1979 and was the work of Frank

102

Spaven who, from 1966 to 1977, had been head of the board's Planning and Research Division. It appeared in the board's own publication, *A Contemporary Account*, which attempted to set out 'background information about the Highlands and Islands of Scotland'.[2]

Spaven was able to conclude,

> The board, since 1965, has achieved radical improvements in providing local jobs and tackling depopulation through the capacity of local people and the interest of outsiders in starting new enterprises. Since 1971, in some areas and for the time being, oil-related industries have made massive contributions to this result. The once peripheral Highlands and Islands have been 'put on the map' of Britain and NW Europe as never before and the prospects for more people to make a good living in it are much brighter than they were, provided development assistance through the board and infrastructure through the local authorities are continued in the non-oil areas and in the post-oil era.

To back this conclusion he drew support from the amount of financial assistance provided by the board (then totalling £53 million), the number of projects helped (4600), the employment provided (around 13,200 new jobs) and the pattern of population change (for the first time in over a century, the Highlands and islands had recorded an inter-censal increase in population in the 1971 census). He also acknowledged that problems existed; depopulation continued in many small, rural communities, he pointed out, and unemployment rates had begun to rise again.

Both writers chose to ignore some issues which many would regard as fundamental to any effort to put the board into perspective and, indeed, raised almost as many questions as they answered. Perhaps this limitation was deliberate, even unavoidable, but it serves to illustrate the difficulties of dealing with what was, and remains, a unique organisation.

Paramount to any understanding of the board and its record is an appreciation of the limits within which it works. At its birth it was seen by its midwives, and others, pretty much as Carter described it—a dynamic body on the lines of the TVA. *The New Statesman* hailed it as a measure 'which if properly applied, paves the way for revolutionary change in the seven crofting counties'.[3]

Its founding father, Willie Ross, the Secretary of State, looked upon it as a means of redressing history; the Highlander, he told the House of Commons, was the man on Scotland's conscience.[4] Even as late as 1970 one writer hoped 'that it will become, as Franklin Delano Roosevelt hoped the TVA would become, "a corporation clothed with the power of Government, but possessed of the flexibility and initiative of private enterprise" '.[5]

Such high hopes were present, too, in the board's headquarters in the early days. They were responsible, in the main, for the influx of staff from the world of commerce and industry who, once they got down to work, were confused by the contrast between the rhetoric and what they found in practice. Had they listened to what Michael Noble, the previous Tory Secretary of State, had had to say in the second reading debate about the provisions of the bill which established the board, they perhaps would have been less innocent.

Claiming that the board was being given less power than any other body, he said, 'This board has not got one tooth, but the Secretary of State for Scotland has got a most ferocious set of snappers.' If the board was to be of any value it would have to have a great deal more independence than Mr Ross had given it.[6] With these few words he put his finger on the major limitation on the board's freedom of action—the controlling hand of the Scottish Office. The board was not, and is not now, the independent agency of popular belief.

Complete freedom of action, of course, never was a practical possibility. The board is responsible ultimately to the Secretary of State and, therefore, must be subject to control by his civil servants. Initially this was secured in quite personal terms. The board's first secretary, or chief of staff, Bobby Fasken, was a civil servant and remained on secondment from Scottish Office for the first few years of his appointment. His deputy and his senior administrative officer were also civil servants of long experience.

The fact that the first chairman, Bob Grieve, had enjoyed a successful career in the public service meant that there was no real risk of the board adopting an entirely commercial profile. Indeed, common advice to officials proposing initiatives was that, whatever was done, the board must not embarrass the Secretary of State.

An additional check on the board's behaviour was the presence at its meetings of an official representative from its sponsoring department, DAFS. Though this practice ended eventually, the same end was gained by the submission of the minutes of the board's discussions and decisions to St Andrew's House. It took the board some time to learn what to record and what to omit from these documents.

In any event, no matter how cleverly it boxed or how fast its footwork, it was subjected to major controls over the only resources it had, its staff and its budget. Initially, it could not hire any one, not even the lowliest clerk, without the approval of DAFS. Through time this regulation was relaxed but, even now, the board cannot appoint, of its own accord, staff to its most senior ranks. In essence this meant from the beginning that Scottish Office decided not only how many staff the board should employ but also, in terms of salary, what its quality should be.

Bob Grieve explained the difficulty to Robert Maclennan in 1969, 'We do feel that we might have more elbow room in increases in staff for particular purposes and perhaps particularly in being able to fix the remuneration since we are so much a commercially aligned body, and we have to compete, of course, with the outside world pretty strenuously to get the right kind of staff.' The board, he added, would have liked to offer competitive salary rates 'in particular cases if we think that that is the only way to get the man of the quality that we require to do the job'. It was admitted that the board had encountered some difficulty in attracting staff of the right kind because of that problem.[7]

Though, broadly speaking, the board was able to shape its organisational structure, it found these restrictions no light rein. For each addition to its complement the board had to make its case and wait on the judgment of the centre. The same procedure was followed on the annual budget.

Divisional heads would begin it by making individual bids to cover what they considered would be their workload over the forthcoming year. Subsequent discussion adjusted these to bring out a total about which there was general agreement. At that stage the bids were submitted to a formal board meeting for further examination and, eventually, approval. Thereafter discussion took place between the board and its sponsoring department at Scottish Office, at first DAFS, then SDD and now SEPD. It is on the last named's vote that the board's budget is borne.

They, in turn, negotiated their own departmental bids within Scottish Office's overall total so that, finally, the board's claim would go forward to the Treasury at the beginning of the public expenditure cycle as a small part of the Scottish Secretary's share of the Government's total spending plans.

Throughout this long process many factors, some of them clearly extraneous, would affect decisions about the board's budget. At no time, however, was the board allowed to make its case direct to the Treasury. Fortunately, though those circumstances could create real problems, the board did not suffer in general for a lack of finance; indeed, it was able on occasion to secure additional resources. Like other agencies, of course, it suffered at times of restricted public spending but its common experience was to find it was in danger of not spending its total approved budget.

In the calendar of the public service that is the gravest sin, and it carries a heavy penalty. What is not spent is returned to the Treasury maw never to reappear. For the board there was no way in which the balance could be carried forward to the next financial year; nor was there a means by which, on its own, it could switch approved funds from one of its programmes to another. Until 1980 such flexibility had to have the prior agreement of Scottish Office.

Such limitations clearly lead to many unnecessary complexities, particularly on schemes, like factory building, which run for several years, and to some abuses. It is a frequent phenomenon in public agencies to see purchases rise dramatically in the closing month of the year simply to prevent the money thus spent being 'lost'.

Scottish Office's control of the board is tightened further by the formal conditions which it attaches to the finance it provides. A copy of these is at Appendix 2. Providing the basic ground rules within which the board is expected to work, these are some of the 'snappers' to which Michael Noble referred in 1965.

Ferocious they may be, as he claimed, but the sharpest are provided by the fact that the senior civil servants in New St Andrew's House always stand between the board and its political master, the Secretary of State. This gives them ample scope to use their influence and it is a capacity which they are not reluctant to exploit.

At the time of the hullaballoo over the board's plans for Moray Firth Development, for example, they instructed the board not to speak publicly nor respond to press queries without first clearing its remarks with the department. More importantly, with the Uist bulb scheme they set a condition for their approval which could not be met. Much later, when the board was anxious to augment its powers over rural land use, they either misled the board or misunderstood the view of their ministers on the question of whether the board would have to demonstrate the ineffectiveness of its existing powers; further, they appeared to delay seeking a political answer as the likelihood of a general election became stronger.

It is fair to say that, through time, the bonds were loosened; the financial limit within which the board works on its own, for example, has risen from the original £25,000 to £250,000. But it remains the case that on key issues of policy and major projects the bonds are as tight as ever they have been. Power continues to reside in Scottish Office.

John Robertson, who resigned over that fundamental issue, or rather because of the problems which he detected flowing from it, had an early, informal illustration of that fact. During a reception in the board's offices for George Willis, then the junior minister at the Scottish Office responsible for Highland affairs, he took part in a discussion with the minister about the plans for improving the main routes to the north. It had been suggested that priority ought to go to improving the southern approaches to Dundee rather than those to Perth. No, no, George Willis assured his listeners, 'they' were adamant that the Perth crossing had the greater urgency.

Figure 11.   Cooperative café, Iodair, North Uist

'They?' said Robertson. 'They? I must say I get worried when I hear a minister of the Crown referring to "they" and "them".'

By contrast, politicians rarely had a direct influence on board policy in the sense of securing the rigid application of their particular philosophy. There was one exception. Following Edward Heath's victory in the 1970 election, when the government still was gung-ho on free enterprise, Patrick Jenkin, then at the Treasury, advised his Scottish colleague, Gordon Campbell, that he ought to see to it that the board sold Gaelfish, its fish processing company in Stornoway. The Scottish Secretary duly passed on the instruction.

The plant was losing money and, though profits were in sight, buyers clearly were not thick on the ground. If the board complied with the government's dogmatic assertion, then the chances were that it merely would add to the number of unemployed on Lewis. But Scottish Office insisted.

At a meeting in Inverness Sir Andrew Gilchrist, the board's chairman, explained the difficulties to Gordon Campbell. He urged that the board be given more time to comply with his wishes. A few weeks only—if these were not granted then the end result would be redundancies just before Christmas. It was a strong argument and tellingly made. The Scottish Secretary appreciated its validity but, he said, he could give no decision until he had cleared it with colleagues in London. Though this need to check with Whitehall about so minor a matter illustrates the lack of will from which Scottish Secretaries can suffer, in this case the board's request for extra time was so sensible that it could not be refused. But eventually the factory was sold and the only reason for the sale was the government's political philosophy.

To describe this episode as an exception should not obscure the fact that the complexion of the administration—and the board has worked to Scottish Secretaries of both main political parties—always was a major consideration in the board's mind. Sir Andrew Gilchrist, for example, thought it would be a waste of time to pursue the land issue while a Tory Government was in power but, more generally, the board applied self-censorship. Proposals were shelved because they were perceived to run against the political grain or were re-shaped so that they would run with it.

These were the general constraints within which the board worked and continues to work. Although its founding act seemed to imply otherwise, it was never possible for the board to become a Highland TVA; the detailed administration and interpretation of the legislation were a brake on any such ambition.

In putting the Highlands and Islands Development (Scotland) Act on the statute book in 1965, Parliament gave the board two main objectives; first, it was to 'assist the people of the Highlands and Islands to improve their economic and social conditions'; and, second, to 'enable the Highlands and Islands to play a more effective part in the economic and social development of the nation'.

No attempt was made to quantify these targets. Using them, therefore, as yardsticks by which to judge the board's work is fraught with difficulties. These are complicated further by the fact that the board was given only one practical means by which to accomplish its objectives—its ability to provide finance for development.

It could not operate directly on many of the factors which go towards constructing the 'economic and social condition' of a community. It had no planning powers, these being retained by the local authorities; it could not invest in roads or build houses or erect schools. Certainly it was able to, and did, carry out research into associated fields. It could be argued that its early work in the Moray Firth area, through the report of the Jack Holmes Planning Group, gave the local councils an advantage in coping with the consequences of major growth which otherwise they would not have had. But the fact remains that the board's power was limited to supporting and encouraging productive enterprise.

By that yardstick the board's record seems an impressive one. The table on p 110, gleaned from the board's annual reports, shows that in the period from 1965 to 1980 it gave financial assistance to 7059 projects worth over £80 million (at original cost) and that these schemes were expected to create or retain 21,073 jobs.

These bald statistics, of course, hide as much as they reveal. They do not show, for example, how many jobs were skilled or unskilled nor whether the projects were confined to an essentially local market or contributed to national exports.

As Carter realised, published statistics never were the board's strong point. Even in 1980 when apparently more sophistication was applied to their production there remained gaps which prevent the emergence of a proper evaluation. The board itself seems to have admitted to such difficulties and concentrated its statistical report on the period 1971 to 1980, a confession perhaps that, in retrospect, figures for the earlier years were too suspect to be relied upon.

The main sectors on which the most recent figures shed light are:

POPULATION From the beginning this was a vital yardstick for the board and its sponsors. Bob Grieve explained that, in all the solutions offered to him and his colleagues in the first few months of the board's life as ways in which to tackle the Highland problem, there was one common element—to stop the drift of population away from the Highland counties. That was adopted as one of the chief objectives. The 1971 census suggests that it had been achieved very quickly. For the first time in over a century an increase in the population was recorded—from the 304,000 of the 1961 census to over 307,000. Of course, there is no way to prove beyond doubt that it was the board's work which had caused the historic reversal but the coincidence of the events is striking. From 1971 that trend has been maintained with the population in 1980 being estimated at 325,000, representing a yearly change throughout the decade of plus 0.97 per cent. Unfortunately the picture is not consistent throughout the area; in those parts of the Highlands and Islands with few development opportunities and which had been unaffected largely by the incursion of the oil industry, the drift remained apparent. In the ten years from 1971, in Sutherland, Caithness and the Western Isles population fell. The last was of most significance for Grieve had defined experience there as the litmus test of the board's efforts. In its first report he had recorded: 'No matter what success is achieved in the Eastern or Central Highlands . . . the board will be judged by its ability to hold population in the true crofting areas.'[8]

	No. of projects	Total assistance* £m	Jobs created/ retained
1965–6	176	0.83	1024
1967	311	1.4	1115
1968	417	2.3	1274
1969	229	1.1	728
1970	305	1.9	1280
1971	406	2.7	1156
1972	558	4.5	1649
1973	400	3.4	1861
1974	448	5.0	1093
1975	419	5.3	987
1976	499	6.4	1100
1977	726	8.8	1266
1978	782	13.2	2000
1979	846	11.1	2900
1980	737	12.3	1600
1965–80	7059	80.2	21,073

* At original cost

UNEMPLOYMENT   In 1971 the rate of unemployment in the Highlands and islands was 7.9 per cent; by 1980 it had moved up to 9.1 per cent. This suggests that, on the face of it, the board was running very hard to stand still. It should be remembered, however, that it operates only on the margin; of much more significance in employment terms during these years were the investments of the oil companies and the firms which serviced them which, by 1980, had produced over 17,500 jobs in the area, and the expansion of the service sector which, in part, was a response to the oil developments and to the reorganisation of local government in 1975. In the six years to 1977 alone, employment in that category leapt by nearly 14,500. Compared with such magnitudes the board's efforts to help create around 1300 jobs a year are of smaller importance particularly if, as is accepted, that figure is overstated by about 20 per cent. In relative terms, however, the pattern of employment in the area improved quite markedly throughout the seventies, as the following figures suggest.

UNEMPLOYMENT (per cent)

	1971	1979	1980
Highlands	7.9	9.0	9.1
Scotland	5.7	8.0	10.0
Great Britain	3.5	5.6	7.3

While the Highlands and islands shared the vicissitudes of the national economy they were able to cope with them relatively better. Though there is no firm evidence to prove the case, this may have been due to the presence of the board which was able to keep several firms afloat during rough economic waters. A major influence, without doubt, was the presence—particularly in Shetland, Orkney and around the Moray Firth—of the oil industry and its suppliers.

STRUCTURE OF EMPLOYMENT   'Manufacturing industry is the third main prop (of the Highland economy),' said the board's first report, 'and we increasingly regard it as the most urgent of all relative to the immediate need to stem a substantial proportion of the emigration of talented sons and daughters from the Highlands and islands. . . . Without it, the region will continue to lack any real possibility of a substantial enough rise in numbers to give credibility to Highland regeneration.' At the time at which these words were written the proportion of the working population engaged in manufacturing was about 11 per cent; by 1971 it had risen to 13.3 per cent and by 1977, the latest year for which figures are available, to 13.5 per cent. Though the change was small it was occurring when, in the world outside the Highlands, the general trend was in the other direction. This, in part, must have accounted for the apparent strength with which the regional economy resisted the recessions of the seventies which kept their sharpest edges for manufacturing industry.

BOARD INVESTMENT   Between 1971 and 1980 the board invested over £118 million (at 1980 prices) in development projects, 58 per cent of it by way of loans or equity participation. Nearly 30 per cent of the total was directed to the tourism industry, which attracted twice as much in grants as it did in loans; indeed more than one fifth of all the board's help during these years consisted of grants to toursim enterprises. The sum was just £4 million short of the total assistance given to manufacturing. Though this might suggest that the board did not practice what it preached, it is more a simple reflection of reality. Manufacturing is neither an obvious nor an easy activity in the Highlands and islands though, contrary to general opinion, the area does have a long industrial history; by contrast, tourism offers many opportunities and, from the board's point of view, it was a case of exercising choices as well as control. In farming, the Highlands and islands did not escape the effects of the movement away from the land experienced in the industrialised countries of the world. During the early seventies jobs were disappearing from the region's agricultural industry at a rate of about 130 a year while board-assisted ventures were creating around 110 annually. Investment in fishing, on the other hand, brought direct gains in employment on boats and in boat building and fish farming. In terms of cost per job it was the most expensive at over £15,500; land was next highest at £10,000 with tourism at £7800 and manufacturing cheapest of all at £3300.

Revealing though they are, these statistics do not provide satisfactory guidance as to whether the board was making progress towards the objectives of improving the social condition of the Highlands and of enabling the area to play 'a more effective part in the social and economic development of the nation'.

To a great extent, searching for such evidence in relation to the social objectives would be unproductive. The areas in which it would be found—health, education and crime rates, for example—are far beyond the board's sphere of influence. Even in such matters as transport and housing the direct responsibility lies with central and local government. The link between the economic and social aims is provided, as the board initially realised, by population numbers; the greater the population, the stronger the argument for improvements in social infrastructure. This factor clearly has been at work in the Highlands and islands during the past 15 years, as, for example, the expensive improvements to the A9 route from Perth northwards clearly testifies.

In a direct sense the board's work was felt in the social sphere only at the margins. It helped remote communities achieve television reception, it provided finance towards Eden Court Theatre as well as the setting up of Radio Nan Eilean in Stornoway and helped during the early years of the *West Highland Free Press*. For nearly all of its first decade it took an ambivalent attitude to the Gaelic culture of the west coast and the islands, arguing that a strong economy was a pre-requisite of a healthy language.

The formation of the Western Isles Islands Council in 1975 was of much more consequence to Gaeldom though the board did give financial backing to some of the council's initiatives in the fields of drama, publishing and education. Its later encouragement of community cooperatives demonstrated that it still held to the view that jobs and incomes had first priority.

There can be little doubt that the board did help the people of the Highlands and islands 'to improve their economic conditions'. By concentrating on investing in productive enterprise it strengthened the regional economy, particularly in fishing, farming and tourism. Whether this, in turn, enabled the Highlands to play a more effective part in the economic development of the nation cannot be answered satisfactorily.

A great deal of research is required into the relationships between the Highland and the national economy. It is quite evident that, from about 1971, the region has played a key part through its proximity to the country's oil wealth. The only other sector of which that can be said without fear of contradiction is fishing where, in both the traditional hunting and the new farming sectors, the Highland and islands share of the national product outstrips by far what would be expected in terms of population proportions. The board, of course, has had a direct and telling influence in that sphere although the same is not true of oil.

That fishing, agriculture and tourism are healthier industries than otherwise they would have been is not the same as saying that the burden of expenditure by central government in the Highlands and islands is lighter as a consequence. Indeed, all the evidence suggests that these sums are much higher and, in some instances at least, they are so because of board activity. 'Taking the Highlands off the back of the nation' never was a realistic objective for the board, attractive though the proposition appeared to politicians in the Central belt of Scotland.

But it was not only MPs in Harold Wilson's first administration that set the board objectives. Outside the House of Commons, radical opinion had great expectations.

These found expression in the work of a special committee which was set up in the early 'sixties to prepare a Scottish policy for a confidently expected Labour Government. Chaired by Judith Hart, it had among its members Ken Alexander and Roderick MacFarquhar. For Highland affairs their main recommendation was the setting up of a development authority.[9]

There was some disagreement about the structure of the proposed body. MacFarquhar argued that it should be small in number and that its members should be appointed by the Secretary of State. Alexander took almost the opposite view, proposing that the new authority should take over from Government and other agencies 'those functions essential to economic and social planning of the region'. It would be given planning powers and would have the task of preparing a development plan for the Highlands and islands whose residents would have representatives—elected directly or indirectly through their existing authorities—on the new body.

Neither view totally won the day. The board was much bigger than MacFarquhar had suggested and was able to engage the specialist staff which Alexander had seen as a 'first essential'. The democratic element, if it existed at all, was relegated to the Consultative Council, part of the membership of which consisted of nominees from the local authorities. In practice the body which emerged was fairly close to the MacFarquhar model, although not accepting its recommendation on staff.

In a paper, used by the Secretary of State during the debate on the bill's second reading, MacFarquhar suggested that 'a reasonable population target figure for 1985 would be probably 300,000'. That his proposed total had been passed by 1980 must have proved as pleasing as the fact that the board had had little choice, when it came to it, but to follow the general prescription on which the committee had agreed.

This was drawn upon by Ken Alexander in an article in the *New Statesman* in October 1965, a month before the board got down to work.[10] Where Roddy MacFarquhar's paper had said that there were only two classes of industry that could be considered suitable for the High-lands—basically food processing and those with products which had a high value relative to their weight—Alexander wrote, 'Manufacturing industry can never provide the main field of employment in the Highlands. Distances that are too great and population densities that are not great enough, together prevent most industries from enjoying the internal and external economies of scale necessary for competitiveness.'

Fifteen years later the board would have no cause to disagree with either of these statements. But it had failed to live up to the expectations of the committee in two central areas.

The first was in planning. The committee had assumed that one of its major tasks would be to devise a plan for Highland development. This the board never produced, despite a return by Alexander to the idea in the course of a speech to conference in Inverness organised by the Scottish Trades Union Congress in 1968—indeed despite the five years in which he was chairman of the board.

Its absence was due as much as anything to the approach of its first chairman, Bob Grieve. Superficially at least, this is surprising. Grieve had been chief planner at the Scottish Office and had been a key figure in that department's contributions to the Government's planning initiatives in the early 'sixties. But, as he was later to admit, by the time he took up his appointment as chairman of the board in 1965, he had lost faith in planning. What was required was a broad strategy which gave the board as much elbow room as possible; a detailed plan, in his view, could be inhibiting, preventing responses to development opportunities as well as to crises.

Ken Alexander became chairman in 1976, shortly thereafter giving an indication that his enthusiasm for planning had waned since his challenge to Bob Grieve eight years earlier. What had been the board's planning and research division became, under a new head, its policy and research division, with both its strength and its role increased.

By 1979 he was able to write, '... It is essential to bear in mind that the Highlands and islands is not a uniform area and that policies for development cannot, therefore, be tailor made to one model.'[11] Thus the Labour Party committee's argument for a single development plan for the region eventually bit the dust.

But, though important, that was not to be their central disappointment. This came without question on the land issue.

In his seminal paper to his Labour Party colleagues in the early 'sixties Roddy MacFarquhar devoted a great deal of attention to land, arguing that without some breakthrough there would literally be no hope 'that people will return to the Highlands, or that the young and vigorous will be encouraged to stay'.[12]

He also supported the view set out by Margaret MacPherson in her note of dissent in the report of the Taylor Commission in 1954. This read:

I came, therefore, reluctantly and regretfully, to the conclusion that I could not sign a report which, in its final form, did not go far enough to remedy the evils of which we had all become aware.

My colleagues propose the appointment of a commission whose duty it will be to supervise and control crofting land, leaving ownership as at present in private hands. I am convinced, however, that crofting can never stand on its own feet until the nation owns all crofting lands. This, I believe, is the only way in which control and supervision can be real.[13]

The gap between aspiration and achievement was vast. Though throughout its first fifteen years the board always had at least one member who was sympathetic to these claims—Prophet Smith, Bill Scholes and latterly Ken Alexander himself all shared MacFarquhar's political stance—it avoided the challenge. Its policies tended to reinforce rather than weaken the *status quo*.

By 1980 there were signs that the board was running out of steam. Morale among its staff was low. Ministers had been unable to find a successor to Ken Alexander who had resumed his academic career; the Secretary of State had been compelled to persuade David Dunbar-Nasmith, Alexander's deputy, to hold the fort until a new chairman could be appointed. He also was forced, because the board's statute required it to have four full-time members, to give the secretary a temporary extra role by appointing him a member for an interim period.

George Younger, of course, also had rejected the board's case for strengthening its powers over rural land use, a blow which the board had absorbed without even a whimper. But there were other reasons for the board's apparent loss of direction. Its innate tendency to bureaucracy had been not so much held in check as encouraged. The balance of its limited manpower resources had been pushed in favour of administration and the trend had been accelerated by decisions to allocate further staff to research and administrative activities. The creative edge of the organisation was blunted. Two developments both illustrated and contributed to this growing loss of purpose.

The first was the hiring of Venture Founders Corporation of Boston, Massachussets, to seek out for the board entrepreneurs capable of starting and running fast-growing, multi-million pound businesses. This decision, not reached easily or at small cost, caused concern among some staff. According to them the US consultants were being hired at substantial cost to the public purse to do a job in which they already were expert and which, as board employees, they regarded as theirs. The board's view was that any new technique was worth trying and that, in any event, it did not have the staff resources which could be directed so intensively to the one end.

By any yardstick that was the call of despair. It suggested that in fifteen years the board had learned nothing about its basic task of encouraging investment in the Highlands; or had learned enough to know that it had built itself into an organisation that was not capable of doing it. Either way it was folly because it undermined the view the board's staff took of themselves.

But the board persisted with the notion. Eventually, late in 1981, the first fruit of the endeavour and of the hard work put into it by both the US experts and the board officials assigned to them was announced. This was a project to be developed by an entrepreneur who had been assisted financially already by the board and with whom it had been working for at least four years.

No razzamatazz had been required, no great publicity, no fat fee—simply a quick check in the board's own files.

The second development had been decided earlier and had concerned the location of the board's own project, Highland Craftpoint. This had been seen as a fundamental issue by Prophet Smith before he retired.

> To my mind, [he wrote in a farewell memorandum] this project is the crucial one for the board. Should the board disregard the geographical implications of where you train young people from the west and decide to locate the centre in the south east or east of the area then a crucial decision will have been made. The board will have implicitly thrown out the concept of a balanced development throughout the region. . . .
> It would be the final throw for all those who are interested in a prosperous and balanced industry throughout the whole of the Highlands and islands. . . . This is the crunch issue to demonstrate exactly where the board stands on the distribution of new industry.[14]

His advice went unheeded and Craftpoint went to Beauly, within fifteen miles of the board's head office in Inverness.

Such decisions seemed to negate the board's own philosophy and action. They did little to reassure its staff and its supporters who already were spending time worrying about the growing public concern over the apparent duplication of effort by various bodies in the field of development. In that they were not alone.

Highland Region asked the Institute for the Study of Sparsely Populated Areas late in 1978 to study the concurrent functions of public authorities in the region. The Institute's report, published in December 1979, contained some evidence of duplication and waste and suggested, among other things, that methods of coordination between the various bodies needed improving.[15]

The report was greeted with a blast of blistering criticism from the board which claimed that the report suffered from both general and specific inadequacies.[16] Nevertheless, even if it had had no value at all, the issue of concurrent functions remained.

The issue was given real point by the presence and growing strength of the Scottish Development Agency and the Scottish Tourist Board, neither of which, of course, had existed when the board was established. Working relationships with each of them were controlled by a set of mutually agreed guidelines which also had the blessing of the Scottish Office.

So long as these guidelines tried to minimise areas of possible conflict and duplication there would be less likelihood of political action to change the existing structure. Even for a Conservative Secretary of State to diminish the board's functions would be a formidable risk. But the reality was that neither the SDA nor the STB could consider themselves national bodies so long as, in over half the land area of Scotland, they had to defer to a regional organisation. They would be the exceptions in the world of the quango if they rested content.

What was certain was that the original justification for the HIDB had been eroded. That had been based on the observation that the Highland problem was 'special' and, therefore, required a 'special' solution. No longer was that distinction so clear. Oil had blurred it and had helped ensure that the Highlands and islands stood up better to the economic rigours of the seventies than other parts of Scotland. The deep recession which began the new decade recognised no convenient administrative boundaries.

In that circumstance no area was special and every region needed 'special' help. The board itself had contributed to removing the distinction by acquiescing in its defeat on the land issue, which always had been a central part of the Highland problem. By refusing to join battle on the ground that really mattered, it could claim no essential or special difference between its industrial and tourism promotion functions and those of the SDA and the STB—nor could it advance the Highlands and islands as being in special need of them. It was, it seemed, in no condition to cope with the biggest psychological blow it ever had suffered.

On 14 October 1981 the price of shares in the British Aluminium Co. fell on the Stock Exchange by 7p to 31p. The City buzzed with rumours that BA was about to close its smelter at Invergordon. The company's finance director told The Scotsman that there was no present intention of closing the smelter either temporarily or permanently. 'The company have made no firm decision yet on the future of the smelter,' he said.[17]

A few days before, representatives of the firm had told officials of the Department of Industry that BA's position was serious and that there was a possibility of its pulling out of Invergordon. From mid-November a team of civil servants, led by Gavin McCrone of the Scottish Economic Planning Department, attempted to negotiate a new deal with the company which would allow it to keep the plant running.

Throughout, BA insisted that only a fresh power contract, guaranteed until the end of the century with no review clauses, would be sufficient. At the beginning of December Ronald Utiger, the company's chairman, told the Scottish Secretary, George Younger, that the smelter was bleeding the group to death.

A package which doubled the subsidy the firm already enjoyed on its electricity supply and which would cost £16 million a year was put together by officials. The cost, and the absence of any provision for regular review, were enough to ensure that Cabinet Ministers could not accept it. From then on it was a case of negotiating a settlement with BA that would allow it to disentangle itself from Invergordon without causing too much damage to its other interests.

On Tuesday 29 December the company announced 'with great regret the closure of its Invergordon smelter'. The losses it was incurring were so large that they endangered its other operations and thus left the company with no alternative. Its statement went on

> British Aluminium is deeply concerned over the effects of the closure on its 890 employees at Invergordon. However, continued operation of the smelter would have seriously threatened the whole British Aluminium Group with 2,700 other employees in Scotland and 4,500 elsewhere in the UK. Talks on closure arrangements and redundancy terms will begin immediately with representatives of the Invergordon employees. British Aluminium will, of course, cooperate in any efforts to bring new employment into the area by, for example, making land available, and will delay any dismantling of the smelter for at least six months.

The company went on to explain that the power contract, which gave BA rights to take electricity from Hunterston B until the year 2000, had been terminated by mutual consent. 'The residual value of these rights has been agreed,' it said. 'The disputed power charges (which exceeded £37 million at mid year and were the subject of legal proceedings by the North of Scotland Hydro Electric Board) have been settled and balances outstanding on Government loans have been cleared. These loans helped British Aluminium to finance its contribution to the cost of constructing Hunterston B; the balance outstanding at 31 December 1980 was just under £34 million.'[18]

George Younger described the announcement as 'a profound disaster for the area'. The Government had reluctantly concluded that continued operation was not possible without an enormous immediate cost to the taxpayer and a continuing heavy burden estimated at approximately £16 million a year until the year 2000. He decided to provide the HIDB with an extra £10 million over the next three years to enable it 'to undertake special measures to provide new employment opportunities'.[19]

The immediate response to the news was puzzlement and anger. The timing and the abruptness of BA's decision caused dismay that found difficulty in gaining public expression. It was not until after New Year had passed that the heated and pointed questions began to be asked. These concentrated on two central issues; first, the terms of the original power contract agreed between the Government, both Scottish electricity boards and the company before the smelter had produced an ingot of aluminium; and, second, the details of the deal between the same bodies which had preceded the smelter's closure.

On 8 January BA responded to questions on the second point, issuing a statement which set out the main constituents of the agreement.[20] The residual rights which the company had under the original contract—to take power from Hunterston B—had been valued at £79.3 million. From that sum the disputed power charges, now standing at £47 million, were deducted and paid to the NSHEB; a further £12.3 million of loan owed to the Government was repaid.

From the balance of about £20 million the company paid the NSHEB a further £4.5 million 'in the normal course of business' so that it was left with a net £15.5 million. In addition the Government had written off over £21 million which was due by the company to the Department of Industry for loans given in 1968 to allow BA to contribute to the capital costs of Hunterston B.

The Opposition was furious. Bruce Millan, the shadow Scottish Secretary, commented, 'It must be the first time in history that a Government have actually paid a company to close down a major modern manufacturing facility.'[21]

There was a general feeling that all was not what it seemed and that Government Ministers were being less than forthcoming in their comments. George Younger attempted to deal with the situation in a lengthy statement during a debate in the House of Commons on 21 January.[22] His main points were:

1 DETAILS OF CONTRACT
It may help the House if I now explain in rather more detail the provisions of the 1968 contract. Under the contract the company agreed to pay for the construction of some 21% of Hunterston B, in return for a guaranteed supply of electricity for the smelter until the year 2000. 21% of the station was the proportion expected to be required to meet the smelter's demand.

In fact it became clear after the station was commissioned that the output was not going to reach the original design level, and therefore that 21% of the station would not be adequate to meet the company's requirements. Honourable Gentlemen opposite decided in 1976 that it would be wrong to ask the company to acquire the further 5% of the station needed to meet the smelter's demands. Instead the capital cost of this additional 5% was met by the Government through the reimbursements of smelter deficit to the Hydro Board.

2   CHARGES PAID BY BACO

I now wish to explain in rather more detail the power charges which the company was paying, since some confusion on this topic has arisen. These charges were naturally confidential to the parties involved while the contract was in operation, but now that it has been terminated both parties have agreed to their being disclosed. The contract provided for a basic annual charge, to be escalated in line with the cost of replacement fuel at Hunterston B and the operating costs of the station.

It was expected that the charges under the contract would remain at least broadly stable in real terms. In fact the charges have increased in real terms, particularly in recent years as the electricity boards have started to provide for the costs of reprocessing nuclear fuel. Many of the costs associated with nuclear power have turned out to be higher than was foreseen in 1968 when the AGR stations were in the early stages of construction. AGR costs remain, of course, cheaper than the costs of supply from fossil-fired stations, but they are not as low as was originally expected.

The charges actually made to the company in recent years are as follows. In 1980/81 the company were charged by the Board a total of some £18.2m for the contracted supply of 1747m units. When the company's own annual capital and other charges of £3.9m are taken into account its total power costs were some £22.1m, or 1.26p per unit. For 1981/82 the charges provisionally notified to the company in September by Board were some £25.0m. Including the company's own annual capital and other charges of £4.1m this was equivalent to total power costs of some £29.1m, or 1.67p per unit. The company queried certain elements in the increased charges and the Board, after consultation with the Government, offered to adjust the charging formula in a way which would have cut the charges in 1981/82 by some £3.4m while increasing the charges for earlier years by some £2.6m in total. Had this revision been made to the power charge, the company's total power costs, including capital and other charges, would probably have been around £25.7m, or about 1.47p per unit. The final charges would not have been known until the end of the year when the actual fuel and operating costs of Hunterston B were known.

3 RESIDUAL VALUE

I now turn to the so-called 'residual value' provisions of the contract. The contract between the company and the Board, to which of course the Government were not a party, provided for the company to receive, in the event of early termination of the contract, the so-called 'residual value' or the tranche of Hunterston B for which it had paid. I should underline that this payment was provided for explicitly in the contract; it was not a matter over which the Government had any control or discretion. I see nothing surprising or improper in this provision—if two people go into partnership to buy a house, and one of them subsequently decides to move, he is surely entitled to the appropriate share of the value of the house. In the case of a power station, the residual value is the value to the electricity boards of the output expected from the station in the future and this is what BACo were entitled to—the value of the output expected from 21% of Hunterston B from the date of termination until 2000.

4 TERMINATION SETTLEMENT

I spelt out in my statement to the House on Monday the details of the settlement reached between the Government, the Board and the company but as there is still considerable misunderstanding I should perhaps explain it again. The residual value set on the company's share of Hunterston B by the Scottish Boards was approximately £79m. The Board deducted from that sum the charges which the company had been withholding because of the dispute over the interpretation of its contract, so that the company actually received about £32m from the Board in return for surrendering its share of Hunterston B.

The company at the date of termination owed the Department of Industry some £33.5m in outstanding loans. It was clear from the investigations we ourselves carried out into the company's financial position that had the Government required the company to repay these loans in full the company would have been permanently weakened, and would have been obliged to close down at least some of its other operations in the UK, starting with its rolling mill at Falkirk. In view of the threat to the company's other activities, and the large losses it had accumulated at Invergordon over the years for reasons which to some extent were beyond its control, we decided that it would be equitable to waive repayment of approximately £21m of the loans. The company therefore repaid £12m to the Department of Industry out of the £32m it had received from the Board, and retained £20m. The company received that £20m from the residual value settlement, not from the Government. To say, as the rt hon Member for Craigton has stated, that the company received £100m to close down the smelter is a complete distortion of the settlement. The waiving of full repayment of the loans does not guarantee the future of any of the company's remaining plants, and no company is in a position to give such guarantees. What is quite clear is that if we had insisted on full repayment of the loans we would have put several thousand more jobs at risk.

5 IMPLICATIONS FOR THE ELECTRICITY BOARDS

I would now like to turn to the effects of the closure on the Scottish Electricity Boards. These are threefold. They are somewhat complicated and I must ask for the indulgence of the House. Firstly, the Boards will lose the revenue from their largest customer. Secondly the Boards' direct generating costs will be reduced, because electricity demand will be lower. The Boards will respond to this lower demand by reducing the operation of their least efficient stations—the stations with the highest generating costs. This means that the more expensive coal-burning stations at Cockenzie and Kincardine and the oil-burning station at Inverkip will be used somewhat less frequently. SSEB's annual coal consumption will fall by around 750,000 tonnes per annum. The reduction in direct generating costs over the next few years is likely to be greater than the loss of revenue.

Thirdly the Boards will incur additional interest charges, because they have had to acquire the tranche of Hunterston B hitherto allocated to the smelter. The tranche allocated to the smelter amounted to 26% of the station. The company only paid for the construction of 21% of the station but as I explained earlier 26% of the station has had to be reserved for the smelter requirements. It follows that on termination of the contract the full 26% tranche was recovered by the SSEB, with payment for 21% being made to the company and payment for 5% being credited to the Hydro Board's smelter account. SSEB paid £99m to acquire the 26% tranche and the interest charges on this sum will be borne by both Boards because of the operation of their joint generating account.

Taken together these three effects—the loss of revenue, the lower direct generating costs and the higher interest charges—should broadly balance out over the next few years. The Boards are still evaluating the implications in detail and I am not in a position to give any precise estimates. I can assure the House, however, that there will be no significant effects on the Scottish Electricity Boards' tariffs in the near future. In the longer term the savings in generating costs will rise in line with the cost of fossil fuel, whereas the interest charges will remain fixed in money terms, and the overall effect will be to reduce the Boards' total costs.

It has been suggested that the closure of the smelter removes the need for the Board's nuclear station at Torness, which is now under construction. The hon Member for Edinburgh Central has suggested that the closure is a 6-inch nail in the coffin of Torness. 6-inch nails would make little impression on the millions of tonnes of concrete which the Board has poured at Torness. These allegations betray a misunderstanding of the role Torness is to play. The Government have allowed Torness to proceed because it will be very much cheaper to operate than the Boards' oil and coal-fired stations, not because the additional generating capacity will be needed when it is commissioned in 5 or 6 years' time. Over the period of the new station's life the operating savings are expected to exceed by a considerable margin the capital costs of the station. Like the householder who double-glazes his livingroom, SSEB is spending capital to secure lower operating costs. The acquisition of the tranche of Hunterston B hitherto allocated to the smelter has the same effect; in return for the expenditure of £99m SSEB will realise substantial operating savings in the future. But even with the additional nuclear output available from Hunterston B the Board still needs the savings from Torness if it is to hold down the cost of electricity in the 1990s when coal and oil are expected to get increasingly expensive. There is no question, therefore, of the Government seeking to persuade the Board to delay or abandon the Torness project. On the contrary, we attach the highest priority to the station being completed within budget and on schedule, so that the operating savings can start to be realised at the earliest opportunity.

The Board has assured me that despite the recent severe weather conditions the project is still generally on programme and within budget.

6   NEW POWER CONTRACT

I have said that the question of new power arrangements will be one of the subjects to be covered in the HIDB study. I do not wish to anticipate the findings of the study, but a number of proposals have been put forward in recent weeks on which I should make some comment. There is one simple general point to be made. If a new smelter operator at Invergordon were to be treated by the Hydro Board like any other large industrial consumer, the Board would have to charge somewhat over 2.5p per unit in the coming year for its electricity in order to cover the costs of supply. It was evident from the Government's negotiations with BACo that for the operation of the smelter to be economic a price at least 50% below that would be necessary. There are two ways in which this gap can be bridged. Either the Government can compensate the Board for its losses, as was done in the case of BACo, or the costs can be borne by other electricity consumers, as would happen if the Board set aside some of its most economical hydro stations to provide the supply. In fact it would be necessary to set aside some 60% of the Board hydro-electric capacity, because the Board's hydro stations do not deliver their full design output on a continuous basis. There is no escaping the basic choice: the costs would have to be met either by the taxpayer or by other electricity consumers. The amount involved is by no means insignificant; it would probably be of the order of £15–20m per annum, depending on the precise terms of supply. As the joint statement issued by my hon Friend and the Chairman of BACo said: 'Any improved arrangements for a new company would present formidable difficulties, since that contract already provided power at a price approximately half that paid by Scottish consumers.' Nevertheless the Government are ready to discuss with the electricity boards and any potential new operator new arrangements for a power supply for the smelter. The arrangements would obviously depend on the operator involved, the circumstances of their approach to us and the other factors involved.

None of this was a surprise to the board. It had warned the Government the previous June of the impending disaster and had done so several times since, formally in writing and informally in face to face exchanges.[23] It recalled its expressions of alarm as the closure was announced. A prepared statement from its Inverness headquarters said:

> We are dismayed that BA, the Hydro Board and the Government have been unable to reach an agreement which would have enabled the Invergordon smelter to remain in operation. The board has not been party to the negotiations which have taken place, although we alerted the Government to the very serious situation which we have seen developing over recent months and made the strongest possible representations to the Government to find a way to keep the smelter open.
>
> The closure of this major development after only ten years' operation with a consequent loss of 900 direct jobs and many more hundreds indirect jobs is the most serious setback we have suffered in our area since the formation of the board in 1965. The social and economic consequences to the area are so serious that at this stage they are impossible to quantify. Unless some way is found for this smelter to remain open there is little prospect of employment being created in the short term for more than a few of the staff who will be made redundant.[24]

Once more the board appeared to be in a situation where it could not win because of its inherent difficulty of seeming to have responsibility but not having the necessary power. The failure of the smelter had nothing to do with its location or with any other factor over which the board had even a jot of influence. Yet because of the plant's location and because the board had made a strong public case in the sixties for such major investment, the closure was a severe psychological blow to the cause of Highland development.

The board had had no part in either the initial decisions which led to the smelter's presence or in negotiations which had preceded its closure; these had been matters for central Government. The board realised that, if it chose to become involved in any rescue attempt, its own credibility would be put at risk. It was also apparent that it had no real choice. It set to with a gusto that many thought it no longer possessed.

In some respects the board had a strong hand to play. The man who had supervised the building of the smelter and who had managed its operation, Gordon Drummond, was now one of its full-time members. He gave the board intimate and accurate knowledge of the industry in general and of the Invergordon plant in particular. The was backed by the appointment of consultants, who had been hired in early December before the closure announcement to investigate and report on the aluminium industry's prospects.

In the immediate wake of BA's decision the board stated that it was to make every effort to find an alternative user for the smelter and to set up a project team to promote Easter Ross as an industrial location. It also called upon the Government to make Invergordon itself an enterprise zone. Only the second proposition, which the board itself could carry out, seemed appropriate. No matter how well or how strongly it pursued another operator, it was the Government alone which could clinch the deal.

Initially Ministers at the Scottish Office were content to see the board making all the running. This was politically useful though they knew that, when it came to it, they would be the ones who would devise the rescue package and who would have to sell it to the Cabinet. If they were successful theirs would be the credit; if they failed then they could share the ignominy with the board.

If progress were to be made, there were two key issues to be resolved. First was the price which any new operator would pay for its power; the board's consultants suggested that while Invergordon had been paying around 1.7 pence a unit for its electricity its competitors at Anglesey and Lynemouth in Northumberland were meeting charges of 1.3 and 1.0 pence respectively. Second was the price that any new operator would have to pay BA to get its hands on the smelter. Neither would be easy to resolve and neither, of course, was within the board's control. This did not prevent it from trying to influence events.

On power it challenged the Scottish electricity boards. Privately it considered both the NSHEB and the SSEB as having been remiss in carrying out their obligations. Publicly it argued that it was 'already clear that if the Invergordon smelter were able to receive a supply of electricity at the same price as the two other large smelters in the UK do today, Invergordon would be competitive in the European market. If the Scottish electricity generating authorities,' it went on, 'cannot supply electricity to a smelter in Scotland at the same price as a smelter can be supplied in other parts of the UK, then something needs to be done about it, as the English and Scottish grids are joined together. The inter-board agreements and tariff policies require urgent examination.'[25]

It also sought to link the availability of hydro electricity in the Highlands to the possible power contract. 'The natural resources of hydro power,' it claimed, 'should therefore be allowed to play a part in keeping Invergordon and its community alive.'

These were brave, challenging words but they were no more than that. The board was simply the chief of several Highland and Scottish voices that were clamouring for a solution. Appalled as it was by the electricity boards—a view that hardened in the light of its public exchanges with the NSHEB whose chairman, Lord Kirkhill, had tried to deny his board's long held and traditionally favoured social role[26]—it was incensed by the Government's handling of the pre-closure negotiations. It complained that the Ministers' team had failed to secure a fair return for its apparently generous treatment of BA. An opportunity had been missed to get the smelter out of the company's hands so that, despite turning its back on Invergordon and despite agreeing to cooperate in the drive to re-open the plant, the firm remained in a position to exercise a stranglehold over the whole operation.

Ministers were aware, of course, that the board was lobbying vigorously both privately and publicly. While, in the beginning, they had been happy to see the board adopt such a high profile they soon let it be known that too much open argument could jeopardise their delicate political and industrial negotiations. Thou shalt not embarrass the Minister clearly remained the 11th commandment in Inverness and the board fell silent. Away from the public arena it continued to devil away, its officials, for example, working with the SEPD on a joint study[27] aimed at determining the factors relevant to the re-opening of the smelter and assessing other measures which would mitigate the effects of the closure.

At this stage Scottish Office was very optimistic about the prospects of a successful outcome. Ministers and officials based their hopes on what they called the coal option by which a new operator would buy the moth-balled part of Kincardine Power Station and purchase its fuel from the National Coal Board at a price which would bring the costs of its electricity down to the required levels. The proposal was thought to be philosophically clean in political terms and that, therefore, it could be sold to the Cabinet.

Ministers now were making all the running. But they fell at the first major hurdle. It seemed that insufficient preparatory work had been done with Whitehall ministries. Scottish Office, with a great deal of confidence, had based its case on the need to produce a national policy for the aluminium smelting industry on the assumption that the trouble which had afflicted Invergordon was bound, sooner rather than later, to affect the other two plants and particularly the one at Anglesey because, like BA's, it had its power costs linked to a nuclear power station—in its case, Dungeness B. Its assumption was without foundation; Anglesey had a cast-iron saving clause in its contract with the Central Electricity Generating Board which meant it would continue to buy power at a rate which would keep it competitive. There was no need, therefore, for a national policy. The Scottish ministers' case collapsed.

The revelation spoke volumes about the relationship between the Scottish Office and the Department of Energy and posed severe political questions for the Minister of Energy, Hamish Gray, in whose constituency Invergordon lay. It appeared that his officials did not tell him of the Anglesey clause until too late while it seems reasonable to assume that Scottish Office had been asking the wrong questions of them in their official discussions before George Younger and Alex Fletcher took their case to ministerial colleagues.

Hardly had they retreated from that engagement when Mrs Thatcher spurred them to action once more. Following a meeting with a delegation from Highland Region, she said that the 'greatest hope' for a rescue lay with an arrangement by which the plant's power cost would be based on hydro electricity.[28] Since that possibility already had been examined and rejected by the Scottish Office team, it seemed a remarkable claim for her to make. It only made sense if she had not been briefed adequately about the alternatives so that the case, put by the delegation on behalf of hydro, seemed much stronger than it really was.

Not for the first time did the force of the Prime Minister's personality compel members of her political team to pursue a false track. Within a week of the Highland councillors being sent off from Downing Street with smiles on their faces, the Cabinet's economic committee turned down the hydro option.[29] The Chancellor, Sir Geoffrey Howe, Patrick Jenkin, the Industry Secretary, and Nigel Lawson, the Energy Secretary, all rejected it. Expectations that the Government would have some good news to add to the positive announcements it had made during the Hillhead by-election campaign were dashed.

Throughout this period the board had been silent but as the time approached for Scottish ministers to go yet again to their Cabinet colleagues it broke cover. On 27 April Bob Cowan, the board's new chairman, admitted to being 'deeply concerned and disappointed by the Government's inability to find a solution to the power problem'. Time was running out and the potential alternative operators would not wait forever. In a prepared statement to the press he repeated the, by now, familiar argument: the irony of the closed smelter in the area which produced the cheapest power in the UK; the protected position enjoyed by the Anglesey plant; the prospect of a revival in the world aluminium market.[30]

Whether or not the board's intervention, which was claimed to have been carried out without prior consultation with the Scottish Office, carried any weight in Downing Street is not known but, seven days after it had been made, the Cabinet's economic committee approved the framework for a new power contract.[31] Working against a deadline of the end of June, the date at which BA's obligation to keep the plant operational came to an end, the SEPD now was able to talk seriously to the companies whom it considered to be possible operators.

The board, like other authorities in the Highlands and the unemployed in Easter Ross, could do nothing but await the outcome. Throughout it had played all its cards as well as it could, realising from the first that a great deal was at stake. This was not so much a question of its own credibility, though several commentators mistakenly saw it in those terms.[32] Having greeted the initial location of the smelter at Invergordon as a major breakthrough for Highland development it could not see its premature demise as anything other than a fundamental setback to the same cause.

In that strict psychological sense the situation was beyond retrieving, whether the smelter reopened or not.[33] Unfortunately, BA's decision had been but the biggest blow suffered by the Highland economy. Elsewhere the board was directing its energies simply to keeping many smaller companies afloat, sheltering the dim flame of development from the gale of the recession.

Notes

1 *Aberdeen University Review*, vol XLV (1), no 149, Spring 1973
2 A Contemporary Account, HIDB, 1979
3 *New Statesman* 12 March 1965, p 386
4 *Hansard*, vol. 708, Session 1964–5, cols 1079–1204
5 H. McN. Henderson; The HIDB, a British Experiment in Social Engineering, in Government Enterprise 1970 (Stevens & Sons)
6 *Hansard*, ibid
7 Select Committee on Scottish Affairs, Session 1968–9, Minutes of Evidence, 13 October 1969, p 40; HMSO
8 HIDB, First Report, 1965–6, p 5
9 Roderick MacFarquhar kindly gave the author access to these papers
10 Commanding Highlands, *New Statesman* 8 October 1965, p 512
11 HIDB, Fourteenth Report, 1979, p 1

12 Roderick MacFarquhar's papers

13 Report of the (Taylor) Commission of Enquiry into Crofting Conditions, HMSO, 1954

14 'The future', a memorandum from Prophet Smith on his retirement to board members and heads of division, 28 October 1976

15 Concurrent Functions of Public Authorities in the Highland Region; a report for the Highland Regional Council by the Institute for the study of Sparsely Populated Areas, Aberdeen University, December 1979

16 HIDB, Press release 3/80, 30 January 1980

17 *The Scotsman* 15 October 1981

18 British Aluminium, Press release PRO/0900, 29 December 1981

19 *The Scotsman* 30 December 1981

20 *The Scotsman* 9 January 1982

21 Ibid

22 *Hansard,* vol 16, no 40, 21 Jan. 1982, cols 436–506

23 *The Scotsman* 12 March 1982

24 HIDB, press statement, 29 December 1981

25 HIDB, Press release 5/82, 15 January 1982

26 In response to a letter from David Dunbar-Nasmith, chairman of the HIDB, in *The Times* on 13 January, the NSHEB's chairman, Lord Kirkhill, wrote that nowhere in the act which established the Hydro Board was its charter described as 'to exploit the water power resources of the Highlands of Scotland by producing cheap electricity which would help to regenerate the local economy'—the claim made by Dunbar-Nasmith. What he did not point out, of course, was that the words were those used by the Hydro Board itself in its annual reports to describe its function.

27 The Secretary of State, George Younger, announced the setting up of a study by the SEPD and HIDB on 12 January. Its report was published in March.

28 *The Scotsman* 16 March 1982

29 *The Scotsman* 24 March 1982

30 HIDB, Press release 17/82, 27 April 1982

31 *The Scotsman* 5 May 1982

32 This misunderstanding was fairly widespread (Shucksmith and Lloyd in 'The HIDB, regional policy and the Invergordon closure', *National Westminster Quarterly Review,* May 1982, is a typical example) and rested on the belief that the HIDB devoted the bulk of its development effort to large scale, capital intensive manufacturing projects. But the board could not and did not deal with large scale developments like the smelter; these were projects for national decision and national support.

33 In the event the Government's attempts, sweetened by the bait of £100 million of taxpayers' help, to fund an alternative operator came to nothing. It fell to George Younger, the Scottish Secretary, to tell the House of Commons of his failure on July 29, 1982. His decision to set up an enterprise zone at Invergordon seemed hardly sufficient compensation.

APPENDIX 1

Letter to HIDB from SEPD setting out offer of annual grant-in-aid

HIDB GRANT-IN-AID 1981–82

1.   I am writing to offer to the Board net grant-in-aid of £23,597,000 for the financial year 1981–82. This offer is based on estimated gross expenditure of £28,992,000 and estimated receipts of £5,395,000 and is subject to the conditions set out in this letter. It has been announced separately from the Board's recent submission requesting additional provision to which I hope to send the Department's reply shortly.

ALLOCATION OF SUBHEADS

2.   The amounts allocated to individual subheads of the Board's estimates are—

	£
(1) Salaries and Wages	2,544,000
(2) Travel and Subsistence	336,000
(3) General Administration	759,000
(4) Consultative Council	10,000
(5) Research, Surveys and Publicity	1,922,000
(6) Grants and Loans	12,458,000
(7) Projects and Developments	10,963,000
	28,992,000
(8) Receipts	5,395,000
Net Grant-in-Aid	23,597,000

The Department should be informed timeously if there is likelihood of expenditure in excess of the approved figures for those subheads, or of the possibility of significant under-expenditure. Switching between subheads is permitted in accordance with the Department's letter of 14 October 1980.

EXPENDITURE PROCEDURES

3.   The approval now given for expenditure under individual subheads is subject to statutory obligations and constraints, to Government accounting procedures, and to the procedures established for regular consultation about expenditure. The prior approval of the Department is required for—

(a)   expenditure on a new service now falling within the subheads in paragraph 2 of this letter;

(b)   any new long-term commitments or any extension of an existing service within the above-mentioned subheads of expenditure which would involve a large addition to recurrent expenditure in future years;

(c)   any proposals involving possible departure from the principles governing expenditure of public funds, including those pertaining to calling for tenders and award of contracts;

(d)   the write-off of losses and the making of gifts, donations, extra-statutory, extra-contractual, ex gratia or other compensatory payments that are outwith the authority conveyed in the Department's letter of 20 July 1981.

STAFF COMPLEMENT: SALARIES AND WAGES

4.   The salaries and wages subhead of £2,544,000 is based on an overall complement of 249. As such it takes no account of the proposal which has been agreed in principle to second legal staff from Solicitor's Office to work in the Board's offices at Inverness. We hope to settle the financial details of this new arrangement shortly. The Board may create or regrade posts up to SAO and equivalent level provided that the overall complement of 249 and the salaries and wages subhead of £2,544,000 are not exceeded. The Department should be informed of any changes in the Board's staffing structure arising from this delegated authority. A breakdown of staff showing actual numbers in each grade in post and blocked post should be provided when submitting forward estimates for 1982–83.

5.   Salary scales and conditions of appointment remain subject to the approval of the Department and the Treasury; no increases in salary scales should be made without approval by SEPD. The initial appointment of staff must be made at the appropriate minimum or age-point starting salary unless otherwise agreed in advance by the Department.

CONDITIONS OF SERVICE

6.   Rates of travelling and subsistence, including meals and car allowances payable to members and staff of the Board shall be those applicable to the Civil Service. Other conditions of service shall accord with those applicable to the Civil Service unless variations are agreed—or have been agreed—with the Department.

ADVANCES

7.   Advances of grant-in-aid will be made by the Department as required on receipt of an application sent by the *Secretary of the Board* or by the *Head of Finance Division*. All applications must be supported by a certificate in the following terms—

'I certify that the conditions applying to the grant-in-aid have been duly observed in the expenditure of money received to date.'

The Board should not hold large balances in its Current Account and, to facilitate tighter expenditure control, the Department's letter of 12 November 1980 convey authority to the Board to allow a deficit in its Cash Account. Any unspent balances of the grant-in-aid advanced during the financial year will not be liable to surrender but all balances in hand will be taken into account by the Department when examining subsequent applications for advances and fixing the amount of the grant-in-aid for the succeeding year.

FINANCIAL ASSISTANCE

8.   The arrangements governing the disbursement of financial assistance by the Board under Section 8 of the 1965 Act and Section 2 of the 1968 Act are as set out in the document effective from 1 March 1978, as amended by the Department's letters of 2 May 1979, 14 February 1980 and 25 March 1980. The interest rates to be charged to borrowers shall be as notified to the Board from time to time by the Department.

ACCOUNTING

9.   The requirements of Section 13(1), (2) and (5) of the 1965 Act shall be observed by the Board; the books of the Board will be open to inspection by the Comptroller and Auditor General; *and the draft accounts of the Board should be submitted to the Department by 31 July of each year.*

10.   As soon as possible in each month the Board should prepare financial statements in a form agreed with the Department showing (i) for each subhead the expenditure actually incurred in the previous month, the accumulated expenditure to date and the balance available and (ii) additionally under the Grants and Loans subhead, the total of new commitment incurred by the Board in the previous month and the resulting total commitment brought forward.

11.   Copies of the statements required under paragraph 10 should be sent to arrive not later than the 10th day of each month to HT Division, SEPD (Mr J S B Martin), Scottish Office Finance Division 3A (Mr W A Howat), and the Exchequer and Audit Department, Glasgow (Mr D C Somers).

12.   In regard to trading or other revenue-producing businesses or enterprises in which the Board may engage on its own behalf or jointly with other parties, the proposed procedures and form of accounts should be submitted to the Department

for approval. The proceeds of any disposal of property belonging to the Board shall accrue to the revenue of the Board. In regard to the purchase and custody of stores and equipment, the Board shall maintain adequate inventories giving sufficiently detailed information in respect of the stores and equipment that it holds.

MINUTES OF MEETINGS

13.   The Board shall forward to the Department copies of its approved Minutes of Meetings.

ESTIMATES

14.   Estimates of the Board's income and expenditure for the financial year 1982–83 should be submitted to the Department by 30 September 1981. The Board should also submit by the same date revised estimates of expenditure and income for the current financial year showing the balance of grant-in-aid expected to be in hand at 31 March 1982. These estimates should summarise the allocation among the various subheads of expenditure and income and any new subheads which may be proposed.

EXPENDITURE LIMITS

15.   The approved grant-in-aid of £23,597,000 is expressed in terms of out-turn prices, and thus is also the expenditure cash limit.

ACQUISITION OF LAND FOR FACTORY BUILDING AND LEASING OF LAND AND PREMISES

16.   The Board should by 30 September 1981, in compliance with the Schedule of Conditions attached to the Department's letter of 24 February 1978, as amended by the Department's letters of 2 May 1979 and 13 October 1980 provide details of land acquisition and disposal, the building and letting of factories and workshops and such other financial data as is specified in paragraph 6 of Part 1 and paragraphs 4 and 11 of Part 2 of the said Schedule of Conditions prescribed under Section 14(1) of the 1965 Act.

ACCEPTANCE

17.   I should be glad if you would confirm that your Board accepts this offer of grant-in-aid and the above conditions and that it will give effect to them. I am enclosing a copy of this letter for the use of the Board's Finance Division.

APPENDIX 2

ARRANGEMENTS APPROVED BY THE SECRETARY OF STATE AND THE TREASURY TO GOVERN THE EXERCISE BY THE HIGHLANDS AND ISLANDS DEVELOPMENT BOARD OF ITS POWERS TO GIVE FINANCIAL ASSISTANCE TO INDUSTRIAL, COMMERCIAL AND OTHER UNDER-TAKINGS, AND TO SUBSCRIBE TO THE STOCK OR SHAREHOLDINGS OF COMPANIES

INTRODUCTORY

1. The Highland and Islands Development Board (the Board) is empowered by Section 8 of the Highlands and Islands Development (Scotland) Act 1965, read with Section 2 of the Highlands and Islands Development (Scotland) Act 1968, to give financial assistance to industrial, commercial and other undertakings which, in its opinion, will contribute to the economic and social development of the Highlands and Islands. The exercise of this power is subject to arrangements approved by the Secretary of State and the Treasury. The following arrangements have been so approved; they supersede the arrangements issued to the Board in May 1975 and will take effect from 1 March 1978.

2. The Board is empowered by Section 1 of the 1968 Act to form or promote companies and to subscribe to the shareholding or stock of a company, subject to approval by the Secretary of State and the Treasury. The following arrangements include a statement of the conditions under which the Board may subscribe to stock or shareholding.

SCOPE OF FINANCIAL ASSISTANCE

3. The Board may give financial assistance under these arrangements to establish, encourage and support industrial, commercial, agricultural and other undertakings or activities which, in its opinion—

   (a) will contribute to economic and social development in the Board's area;
   (b) will improve employment opportunities in the area;
   (c) are potentially viable; and
   (d) are located wholly or partly within the Board's statutory area.

In these arrangements, such undertakings are termed *economic projects*.

135

4. The Board should obtain the agreement of the Scottish Economic Planning Department before it considers any application for financial assistance for a project located outside its area.

5. The Board may also give financial assistance to projects which have social or partly social objectives but which may not be commercially viable. In these arrangements, such projects are termed *social development projects*.

ECONOMIC PROJECTS
'NORMAL' ASSISTANCE

6. The Board's 'normal' assistance for economic projects should be determined by the application of tests and standards of viablility, of job creation or of job retention similar to those used by SIDAB to determine selective financial assistance given under the Industry Act 1972. A summary of the criteria to be observed in respect of this requirement is at Appendix 1.

7. The Board's 'normal' Assistance may be given in any or all of the following forms of contribution towards capital costs (including working capital):—

(a) *Loans*

(b) *Interest relief grants*
The Board may give loans and interest relief grants on terms and conditions similar to those attached to loans and grants given under the Industry Act 1972; these are set out in Appendix 2.

(c) *Participation in shareholding and stock*
The Board may subscribe to ordinary or preference stock in companies, on the terms set out in Appendix 3.

(d) *Removal assistance*
The Board may give grants towards the removal expenses of undertakings which move into the Board's area, on terms and conditions set out in Appendix 4.

'SPECIAL' ASSISTANCE

8. The Board may give assistance by way of Special Grant in addition to its 'normal' assistance. The criteria to be observed when payment of Special Grant is considered are set out in Appendix 5.

RELIEF OR EMERGENCY ASSISTANCE

9. The Board may give relief or emergency assistance to existing projects which are in financial difficulties, in order to preserve employment and to prevent redundancies. The criteria to be adopted in determining the case for such assistance are given at Appendix 1. The Board shall inform the Department about all cases in which relief or emergency assistance is given.

LIMITATION

10. The Board may give financial assistance (including Special Grant) up to but not exceeding £400,000 in total, and by all forms, for any single project (regardless of the number of applications made in respect of the project).

DELEGATION

11. The Board may give assistance (including Special Grant) up to a total of £250,000 to any one project without the approval of the Department.

12. The Board may give relief or emergency assistance (including Special Grant) up to a ceiling of £50,000 to any one project without the approval of the Department.

13. Applications for assistance for self-contained and individually viable phases of a project may be treated as distinct applications, subject separately to the limits set out in paragraphs 10, 11 and 12 above. Where the initial application for a project is such that the Board may give assistance within the limits of delegation set out in paragraphs 11 and 12 above, the application may not subsequently be considered in separate phases if a level of assistance in excess of these limits is subsequently determined.

ASSISTANCE FOR AGRICULTURE

14. The Board may give assistance for agricultural projects on the terms set out in Appendix 6; these have been agreed with the Department of Agriculture and Fisheries for Scotland.

15. The Board shall consult DAFS or the Forestry Commission, as appropriate, to determine the extent of any assistance offered or applied for from these sources, when it considers applications for agricultural, horticultural or forestry projects.

TOTAL CONTRIBUTION FROM THE PUBLIC SECTOR

16. The Board is expected to encourage applicants for assistance to seek from private sector sources the greatest possible proportion of the funding required for their projects.

17. The total assistance from all sources in the public sector, including Government departments and agencies and local authorities, for any project within the Board's area should not normally exceed 50 per cent of its overall capital cost. Exceptionally, assistance up to a level of 70 per cent of capital costs may be given, provided that the average level of public assistance for all projects in the Board's area does not exceed 50 per cent of the total cost of assisted projects in a given year.

18. For the purposes of paragraph 17 the capital equivalent of factory accommodation provided by Government or local authorities on amortisation loans shall be included as an element of total assistance from public sector sources, but the capital cost of a rented factory shall be ignored. The full amount of all other public sector assistance and 'normal' and 'special' assistance by the Board must be included.

OTHER PUBLIC SECTOR ASSISTANCE

19. It is expected that the Board should be the principal source of selective financial assistance for economic projects located within its area (subject to the limitation in paragraph 10 above). Projects should not normally obtain financial assistance of a discretionary kind concurrently from the Board and from other public sector sources. Exceptions to this general rule are the arrangements approved under the Board's Fisheries Development Scheme; and arrangements for assisting agricultural, horticultural and forestry projects, where the Board may give assistance in addition to that provided for such projects by DAFS (see paragraphs 14 and 15).

20. Where an application for financial assistance of a discretionary nature has been rejected by a Department, or by a statutory body other than the Board, it should not be considered by the Board until after the expiry of 12 months from the date of rejection, unless the Department or statutory body concerned has been consulted and has agreed.

SOCIAL DEVELOPMENT PROJECTS

21. The Board may give grants towards the capital and recurrent costs of projects which are not commercially viable where it is satisfied that they will meet social needs and contribute to social development in its area. Assistance for any single social development project may not exceed £6000, whether paid as a contribution to capital costs or as grant, or series of grants, to recurrent costs.

22. The Board's assistance in the form of social development grants should not exceed £150,000 in any financial year.

23. Before approving a social development grant the Board shall obtain a declaration from the applicant that he has not applied for, nor will apply for, financial assistance from any other public source, except in the case of a recreational or social project assisted by the Scottish Education Department or the Scottish Sports Council, where the Board may give additional loan or grant assistance not exceeding £1 for every £1 contributed from voluntary sources, within the limit of £6000.

TIMING OF APPLICATIONS

24. Subject to the conditions about timing expressed in paragraphs 9(1) and (10)d of Appendix 2, and in paragraph 5(c) of Appendix 5, the Board should normally regard a project as ineligible for assistance on timing grounds if, at the time when a decision falls to be made on eligibility, the establishment of that project has reached a point where it is not commercially sensible for the applicant to withdraw from it.

RETURNS

25. The Board shall provide such information as the Department may request on all applications for assistance, whether these are approved or rejected.

EXCEPTIONS

26. The arrangements set out in the preceding paragraphs govern the administration of financial assistance for industrial, commercial, agricultural, horticultural and forestry projects as well as social development projects within the limits stated. Where the Board considers that exceptional circumstances justify departure from the general or detailed terms of these arrangements, the applications concerned should be referred to the Department together with the Board's recommendations.

(Appendix 1) CRITERIA FOR NORMAL AND RELIEF ASSISTANCE

GENERAL CRITERIA

1. The Board's principal objective in providing normal or relief assistance should be to establish or to support undertakings which are potentially viable and which will maintain or improve employment prospects in its area. The Board should assist projects only where it is satisfied that they will benefit employment, either by creating new jobs or by protecting existing jobs. When considering applications the Board should always identify and examine all the relevant employment implications before determining whether assistance should be offered and in what amount.

CRITERIA FOR NORMAL ASSISTANCE

2. For the purpose of considering applications for normal assistance the Board should establish that the projects concerned fall within one of the following broad categories:

A New projects or expansions of existing projects, which will create additional employment. For these projects the cost per job arising from all public sector assistance should always be determined, and the Board should have regard to the currently accepted cost per job limit used for giving selective financial assistance under the Industry Act 1972. (Where interest relief grant is given, cost per job should be calculated by reference to the notional loan equivalent). B Projects which will maintain or safeguard existing employment (e.g. by installation of new processes or new plant). For these projects it will not normally be possible to establish an exact relationship between assistance and jobs, and the Board should assess carefully all relevant employment factors before deciding the amount of aid to be offered.

RELIEF OR EMERGENCY ASSISTANCE

3. The Board may give relief or emergency assistance to established undertakings, including undertakings which have previously received Board assistance, where all the following circumstances exist:

(a) There is an imminent risk of redundancies (the number of jobs at risk and the timescale involved should be clearly identified).
(b) The number of nature of jobs at risk and the prospects of finding new

employment in the area concerned are such that the loss of employment would be significantly harmful to that area.

(c) The managerial, financial, technical and production resources of the undertaking will be adequate to enable it to continue as a viable enterprise.

(d) The marketing and commercial prospects of the undertaking provide a sound basis for its future viability and for sustaining all or some of the jobs at risk.

4. The Board should have particular regard to the following information when considering relief or emergency cases:

(a) An analysis of the company's current strengths and weaknesses including the quality of management; range of products and share of markets; and the management record. The Board should take expert advice on these matters where appropriate;

(b) Potential viability, including financial projections; identification of principal risks; prospects of business continuing after receivership; and alternative sources of financial support; and

(c) Employment considerations including local unemployment rates; number of jobs at risk; consequential effect on suppliers within the Board's area; and special regional factors.

(Appendix 2) GRANTS AND LOANS UNDER SECTION 8

INTEREST RATES FOR LOANS

1. The Board shall charge interest on loans at a 'broadly commercial rate' or a 'concessionary rate', these rates to be prescribed periodically by the Department.

INTEREST RELIEF GRANTS

2. The Board's interest relief grants shall be at a 'basic rate' and a 'higher rate', these rates to be prescribed periodically by the Department.

FORMS OF ASSISTANCE

3. The Board may assist employment-creating projects (i.e. category A in Appendix 1) by loans at concessionary rates of interest. Where the Board is satisfied that a long lead time will elapse before a project becomes profitable, it may allow an initial interest-free period of up to 2 years.

4. Alternatively, the Board may offer an interest relief grant on funds obtained from private sources. The amount of grant should be determined by reference to the loan which it might otherwise have offered. Where an interest-free period would have been given on a Board loan, interest relief grant at the higher rate may be given for the same period (up to 2 years) followed thereafter by a grant at the basic rate for up to four years. If no interest-free period would have been given on a loan; grant at the basic rate may be offered for up to four years.

5.   The Board may assist employment retention projects (i.e. category B in Appendix 1) by loans at the broadly commercial rate of interest.

LOANS FOR WORKING CAPITAL

6.   The Board may give loans to provide working capital to assist expansion, development or reorganisation. Such loans should normally be recovered over a period of up to 10 years, and rates of interest should accord with paras 3 and 5 above.

SECURITY FOR LOANS

7.   The Board shall obtain the best possible security for any loan in excess of £3000; at its discretioin it may give a loan for less than £3000 without security provided it is satisfied that the loan will be repaid.

GENERAL CONDITIONS GOVERNING LOANS

8.   The Board is expected to adopt the general conditions attached to loans given under the Industry Act 1972; these are set out in the Department's Notes Gencon 1—Public Companies; Gencon 2—Private Companies; Gencon 3—Partnerships, Sole Traders. In addition to these general conditions, each individual loan agreement should set out specified relevant conditions such as the amount to be lent, the terms of repayment, the rate of interest to be charged and the security given.

DETAILED CONDITIONS COVERING LOANS FOR BUILDINGS

9.   (a) *Conditions on which the building is held*

The applicant must own the building site, be in process of acquiring it or hold it on lease with not less than 15 years to run. In the case of a crofter, the building on the croft land must be a permanent improvement in respect of which the applicant would be entitled to compensation under the Crofters Act on renunciation of his croft tenancy.

(b) *Approved cost*

The proposals and cost must be approved by the Board. The approved cost shall include the cost of preparation of plans but not, in the case of premises to be acquired on lease, the rent or other out-goings.

(c) *Schemes eligible*

Applications for loans may be considered towards the cost of:
(i) acquisition of sites and buildings with a view to their improvement;
(ii) the erection of new buildings or the improvement, extension or adaptation of existing buildings.

(d) *Legal documents*

The necessary legal documents shall be prepared by the Board and a charge shall be made for the Board's expenses on a scale to be approved by the

Department. The applicant may apply to have the expenses included in the loan but any additional advice sought by him shall be at his own expense.

(e) *Plans*

Plans should be submitted to the Board for approval with the application and should be to the Board's satisfaction. Planning permission and any other necessary local authority approval should normally be obtained prior to the loan being made.

(f) *Insurance*

All buildings in respect of which a loan is made shall be adequately insured against loss or damage by fire, storm, impact and explosion and consequential loss. This shall be done at the expense of the applicant and with a company approved by the Board. The policy and premium receipts shall be produced for the Board's inspection whenever required and the policy should be suitably endorsed to cover the Board's interest.

(g) *Instalments of loans*

Loans shall be paid to the applicant in such instalments as the Board see fit, with due regard to the progress of work and after such inspections as are considered necessary.

(h) *Repairs*

The borrower shall keep the premises concerned in good repair to the satisfaction of the Board during the period of loan repayment.

(i) *Change in use of premises*

If at any time during the period of repayment the use of the premises concerned is varied, the Board should reserve the right to call in forthwith the balance of the loan outstanding, together with any interest thereon, calculated up to and including the date of such variation.

(j) *Change in tenure*

During the period of repayment, the borrower shall immediately notify the Board of any proposed change in ownership, or of any proposed transfer of an existing lease or sub-lease, in respect of the premises concerned. In such a case the Board should reserve the right to call in forthwith the balance of the loan outstanding together with any interest thereon.

(k) *Period of loan*

A loan shall normally be given for a period of up to 20 years; in exceptional cases it may be extended to 25 years.

(l) *Timing of application*

Applications for a building loan should normally be submitted before work on the building begins. Work may, however, begin at the applicant's own risk before a loan is offered.

CONDITIONS COVERING LOANS FOR PLANT AND EQUIPMENT

10. (a) *Type of plant and equipment*

Loans may be given for any plant and equipment including installation and reconditioning necessary for the carrying out of the business.

(b) *Amount of loan*

The whole cost of the plant and equipment, less any grant but including cost of installation, reconditioning and carriage, may be advanced.

(c) *Duration of loan*

A loan for plant and equipment should normally extend over a period of up to 10 years.

(d) *Timing of application*

Applications for a plant and equipment loan should be submitted before the plant and machinery has been delivered or constructed by the applicant's own employees.

(e) *Insurance*

All plant and equipment in respect of which a loan is made shall be adequately insured against loss or damage. This shall be done at the expense of the applicant and with a company approved by the Board. The policy and premium receipts shall be produced for the Board's inspection whenever required and the policy should be suitably endorsed to cover the Board's interest.

(Appendix 3) SUBSCRIPTION TO STOCK

1. The Board should not use its powers to subscribe to share capital as its principal method of financial assistance.

2. The Board may assist projects by subscribing to ordinary and preference stock on the conditions that:

(a) Subscription to equity be regarded as part of the total assistance given by the public sector to a project;

(b) The Board should not normally take up more than 33⅓ per cent of the issued ordinary shares in a company. In special cases, where the component of other assistance is small, it may take up to 40 per cent; and

(c) The Board should ensure that it obtains legal and financial advice about the standing and the prospects of any company in which it proposes to take a shareholding.

3. Where the Board gives assistance by means of subscription to stock it may exercise the right to nominate a director or directors to the board of the company. The Board shall always secure a right for its staff to have sufficient access to the company's affairs to enable them to submit regular reports to the Board; and the

Board's staff may assist the company in an advisory capacity. The Board shall have continuing regard to the financial standing of the company.

4. Where the Board exercises an option to convert a loan to equity holdings, it shall observe the above conditions.

5. The Board shall take immediate steps to dispose of all shares held in a company, where that company ceases to carry on an undertaking or activity consistent with the requirements of Section 8(1) of the 1965 Act.

(Appendix 4) REMOVAL GRANTS

The Board may give grants towards the following expenses where an industrial or commercial undertaking is established within its area by removal from outwith any assisted area, and where the project concerned will create additional employment:

(a) The cost of removal of plant and machinery, including dismantling and reinstallation within the United Kingdom;

(b) The cost of removal of necessary stock, including raw materials, partly completed and finished foods, spare parts, loose tools, etc. within the United Kingdom; and

(c) Employers' nett statutory redundancy payments made by the company to employees discharged because of the move.

2. The rate of grant paid shall not be higher than 80 per cent of total reasonable expenditure under the headings above. The amount of grant paid shall also be limited by the currently accepted cost per job factor used to determine removal grants given under the Industry Act 1972.

(Appendix 5) SPECIAL GRANTS

1. When considering whether a project should be assisted by way of Special Grant, in addition to normal assistance the Board shall satisfy itself as to all the following conditions:

(a) The project is not likely to succeed on the basis of normal assistance alone;

(b) The project demonstrates reasonable prospects of viability with the special assistance proposed; and

(c) The project is essential to the proper development of the area.

These conditions must be met in all cases.

2. The Board shall have regard to the following circumstances when considering assistance by way of a Special Grant:

(a) Distinct features of the project which demonstrate good grounds for additional assistance, e.g. exceptional need to train workers to new skills, high cost of equipping due to remoteness.

(b) The project is of special significance or has a high potential for generating ancillary enterprises in the Board's area.

3. The rate of Special Grant shall not exceed:

(a) £30,000 (or 50 per cent of the total cost of the project, whichever is the lesser);
OR
(b) a percentage of total costs as calculated below, whichever is the greater.

For the purposes of (b) above, the normal maximum rate will be 20 per cent of the total cost of the project. In the case of projects not covered by Orders II to XX inclusive in the Standard Industrial Classification the maximum rate may be increased up to a ceiling of 30 per cent of the total cost of the project (by one percentage point for every whole thirtieth in the fraction

$$\frac{\text{Cost of Buildings}}{\text{Total cost of Project.}})$$

Where a Special Grant under (a) or (b) includes an element allocated towards the cost of buildings such element shall not exceed in amount 35 per cent of the cost of the buildings.

4. The Board may make the following exceptions to the requirement that Special Grants should complement normal assistance:

(a) Where an application for grant assistance for a project in the service sector is in respect of building costs only, a Special Grant may be offered on its own;
(b) Where a deserving applicant can satisfy the Board that for good reason the conditions attached to the appropriate form of normal assistance cannot all be met by him, the Board may offer a Special Grant on its own, to a limit of £15,000.

5. Special Grants towards the cost of buildings shall be made subject to the following detailed conditions:

(a) *Scale of Grant*

Special Grant towards the cost of buildings shall be in respect of the cost of erecting a building or improving, extending or adapting an existing building. The Board should exclude from the calculation any expenditure which, in their opinion, is not strictly necessary, having regard to the purpose for which the building is required.

(b) *Scope of Grant*

Grants shall not be available for developers erecting buildings for occupation by other persons or undertakings nor shall they be available to tenants in respect of buildings they are renting. Applications from tenants may be considered in respect of adaptions or extensions to existing buildings to be provided at their own expense.

(c) *Timing of application*

Applications for a building grant should normally be submitted before work on the building begins. Applicants should be advised that the Board shall not be committed to work commenced before the grant is offered.

(d) *Plans*

Plans should be submitted to the Board for approval with the application and should be to the Board's satisfaction. Planning permission and any other necessary local authority approval should normally be obtained prior to the grant being paid.

(e) *Insurance*

All buildings in respect of which a grant is made shall be adequately insured against loss or damage by fire, storm, impact and explosion and consequential loss. This shall be done at the expense of the applicant and with a company approved by the Board. The policy and premium receipts shall be produced for the Board's inspection whenever required.

(f) *Instalment of Grants*

Grants shall be paid to the applicants in such instalments as the Board sees fit, having regard to the progress of work, and after such inspections as are considered necessary.

(g) *General*

Grants shall be subject to such conditions as the Board may impose including conditions as to repayment of grant in the event of disposal of the buildings or of the business.

(Appendix 6) CONDITIONS GOVERNING ASSISTANCE TO AGRICULTURE

1. The Board may give loans or interest relief grants for agricultural and horticultural projects. Loan assistance shall be at the 'broadly commercial' rate only (or grant at the 'normal' rate), unless the Board is satisfied that the investment proposed will lead to an increase in employment, or to the maintenance of existing employment which would otherwise be at risk.

2. The Board shall not give grants in addition to a DAFS grant for the same purpose.

3. The Board shall not give loans in addition to a loan from DAFS, or from the Crofters Commission, for the same purpose.

4. A Board loan may be given in addition to a DAFS grant for the same purpose.

5. An applicant may apply for a grant and/or loan from either DAFS or the Board.

6. The Board shall not entertain an application for assistance for a project which DAFS has rejected within the previous 12 months.

APPENDIX 3

UNEMPLOYMENT BY EMPLOYMENT EXCHANGE AREA

1971, 1979 and 1980

	MALES (%)			FEMALES (%)			TOTAL (%)		
	1971	1979	1980	1971	1979	1980	1971	1979	1980
Lerwick	6.4	3.2	2.8	2.6	2.9	3.2	5.1	3.0	2.9
Kirkwall	5.7	6.4	8.2	2.2	5.3	6.1	4.5	6.1	7.4
Thurso	6.5	10.9	8.6	6.8	13.1	12.0	6.6	11.5	9.6
Wick	13.8	11.3	13.2	6.5	11.5	8.6	11.1	11.3	11.1
Dingwall/Invergordon	12.7	9.8	10.2	4.6	16.5	12.7	10.0	11.4	11.1
Inverness	7.5	8.4	8.3	2.2	5.9	5.9	5.5	7.5	7.4
Nairn	9.4	12.1	14.0	3.3	7.7	9.0	6.8	10.4	11.9
Portree	13.4	21.6	20.8	2.7	11.9	11.5	9.1	18.1	17.2
Stornoway	28.3	17.4	18.6	9.0	8.0	8.1	22.1	14.0	14.7
Fort William	5.4	6.6	7.9	5.1	8.9	9.4	5.3	7.4	8.5
Oban	10.7	9.9	9.5	4.0	6.6	7.1	7.9	8.4	8.5
Lochgilphead	5.1	8.8	7.9	3.8	6.2	7.6	4.7	7.7	7.8
Campbeltown	13.0	12.0	12.4	9.2	10.7	12.3	11.6	11.5	12.4
Dunoon	7.2	4.5	7.7	3.2	6.9	8.8	5.3	5.2	8.1
Rothesay	9.3	20.4	18.3	2.4	8.4	9.5	6.2	14.9	14.4
TOTAL HIDB AREA (excluding Arran and the Cumbraes)	10.0	9.4	9.8	4.2	8.2	8.0	7.9	9.0	9.1
SCOTLAND	7.5	9.1	11.3	2.9	6.6	8.2	5.7	8.0	10.0
GREAT BRITAIN	4.8*	6.6	8.5	1.5*	4.2	5.5	3.5*	5.6	7.3

* Includes temporarily stopped
Source: HIDB and Manpower Services Commission

APPENDIX 4

BOARD ASSISTANCE BY SECTOR 1971-80 (at 1980 prices)

	Grants (£)	Loans and shares (£)	Employment created	Employment retained
Land development	3,439,600	11,339,298	894	584
of which: Farm development	1,372,680	8,289,979	361	390
Horticulture	362,323	689,537	143	35
Fisheries	5,808,041	22,012,159	1350	440
of which: Fishing boats	2,314,767	19,574,014	1018	342
Fish farming	3,223,952	1,944,790	273	83
Manufacturing and processing	10,035,389	18,221,673	6502	1845
of which: Fish processing	1,278,693	2,925,784	962	398
Boatyards & marine engineering	620,527	1,306,494	295	195
Crafts	941,187	1,350,690	1175	180
Construction	1,429,683	3,255,098	1317	490
Tourism	24,464,905	10,453,891	3719	754
of which: Hotels	11,714,738	5,332,242	1842	509
Other tourist accommodation	7,341,439	2,591,463	702	93
Catering	1,467,002	782,620	602	16
Recreation and tourist amenities	3,544,868	1,683,297	537	132
Other service industries (excludes tourism and services directly related to land development and fisheries)	3,578,394	3,984,908	1596	339
Total	£48,756,012	£69,267,027	15,378	4452

Notes:

The figures above relate to assistance approved by the board—not payments. Cases withdrawn after approval are thus included. Part-time or seasonal jobs are valued at half a job and part-time seasonal jobs at a quarter.

Source: HIDB.

APPENDIX 5

TOTAL JOBS CREATED AND RETAINED
by board assisted developments since 1971

Years	Total jobs created	Total jobs retained
1971-75	6993	1143
1972-76	7411	1537
1973-77	7664	1889
1974-78	8028	2417
1975-79	8186	3355
1976-80	8533	3309

Note: Part-time or seasonal jobs are valued at half a job and part-time seasonal jobs at a quarter.

Source: HIDB.

APPENDIX 6

POPULATION CHANGE 1971-1980 by local authority areas

Area	1971 Population	1974 Population	1979 Population	1980 Population	Natural Increase 74-80	Est. net migration 74-80	Other[1] changes 74-80	% change per annum 1971-80
HIGHLAND[2]	170,375	178,368	190,507	191,188	+1671	+8485	+2664	+1.29
Caithness[2]	27,779	27,901	27,021	27,033	+141	−966	−43	−0.30
Sutherland[2]	13,634	13,410	13,217	13,168	−319	−309	+386	−0.39
Ross and Cromarty	34,600	38,226	44,502	44,720	+1309	+5015	+170	+2.89
Skye and Lochalsh[2]	9644	9759	10,031	10,121	−267	+287	+342	+0.54
Lochaber[2]	18,674	19,226	20,150	19,962	+311	−357	+782	+0.74
Inverness	49,004	51,897	55,721	56,407	+614	+3569	+327	+1.58
Badenoch and Strathspey	8736	9043	9457	9386	−83	−21	+447	+0.80
Nairn	8304	8906	10,408	10,391	−35	+1267	+253	+2.52
ORKNEY	17,137	17,462	18,134	18,030	−55	+618	+5	+0.57
SHETLAND	17,535	18,445	22,111	22,309	+438	+3687	−261	+2.71
WESTERN ISLES	30,327	30,060	29,758	29,681	−401	+189	−167	−0.24
Argyll and Bute[2]	62,957	64,578	64,262	64,286	−1137	+653	+192	+0.23
HIDB AREA (excluding Arran and the Cumbraes)	298,331	308,913	324,772	325,494	+516	+13,632	+2433	+0.97

Notes:

1 'Other' changes' encompass Forces movements, etc. and any adjustments made to the base year population by the General Register Office to account for more accurate information not available for that year's population estimate calculations.

2 The 1971 and 1974 figures for these areas have been adjusted by the HIDB to make them comparable with the 1979 and 1980 figures which take account of the following boundary changes since the reorganisation of local government:

(a) part of the parish of Glenelg has been transferred from the Lochaber District to the Skye and Lochalsh District of Highland Region;

(b) the parishes of Tongue and Farr have been transferred from the Caithness District to the Sutherland District of Highland Region;

(c) Part of the parishes of Lismore and Appin, Ardchattan and Muckairn and Glenorchy and Inishail have been transferred from the Argyll and Bute District of Strathclyde Region to the Lochaber District of Highland Region.

Source: HIDB and General Register Office, Scotland.

Index